...or sexualisation on young people. Over the past decade, Dr Linda has become one of the most well recognised faces on TV. A regular commentator on psychological issues in broadcast and print media, her comments regarding the psychology behind news and current events are often syndicated by the press and discussed by TV and radio networks both in the UK and the US. Dr Linda is also the resident psychologist for *Cosmopolitan* UK, where her very popular monthly advice column has now been running for twelve years. Dr Linda has a private practice in London, where she lives with her husband and daughter.

About the Author

Dr Linda Papadopoulos is one of the most well-known and respected psychologists working in the UK today. As well as an accomplished academic career, during which she set up and headed successful post-graduate programmes, she is also an active researcher and has published widely in peer-reviewed academic journals. Her work has informed government policy. In 2010, she led a highly acclaimed independent review for the Home Office on the effects

UNFOLLOW

Living life on your own terms

DR LINDA PAPADOPOULOS

piatkus

PIATKUS

First published in Great Britain in 2014 by
Piatkus as *Whose Life is it Anyway?*

Published in Great Britain in 2016 by Piatkus as *Unfollow*

1 3 5 7 9 10 8 6 4 2

A CIP catalogue record for this book
is available from the British Library.

ISBN 978-0-349-405018

**Note: the names of the young women who contributed to
this book have been changed to protect their privacy.**

Typeset in Stone Serif by M Rules
Printed and bound by CPI Group (UK) Ltd, Croydon, CR0 4YY

Papers used by Piatkus are from well-managed forests
and other responsible sources.

MIX
Paper from
responsible sources
FSC
www.fsc.org FSC® C104740

Piatkus
An imprint of
Little, Brown Book Group
Carmelite House
50 Victoria Embankment
London EC4Y 0DZ

An Hachette UK Company
www.hachette.co.uk

www.piatkus.co.uk

Disclaimer

Any recommendations given in this book are solely
intended as education and information. If you have
any concerns about your health and wellbeing, seek
the advice of your GP.

For my Jessie; for my god-daughters
Nadia, Marilena and Belinda
and for Elektra.

Contents

Acknowledgements

So many brilliant twenty-somethings have been integral to the production of this book. A huge thank-you to the wonderful Hannah De Jonk, Rebecca Twomey and Anna Foulsham, who helped me research and collate information, and also, critically, were so generous in sharing their own experiences of navigating the Gen Y landscape. Thanks to the lovely Kara Fitzpatrick, who was a great sounding board, reading early drafts of chapters and sharing her own insights and thoughts about this amazing decade. A huge thanks to Sarah Shea and Stephanie Melrose, the great PR and marketing team at Piatkus, whose infectious enthusiasm for the messages contained in the book, and hard work and creativity in spreading those messages, I am very grateful for.

To Anne Lawrance, my brilliant editor, who got what I was trying to say immediately from our first meeting, and who helped me to write the book I wanted to write – thank you. A big thanks to Anne Newman and Jillian Stewart, the fantastic copy-editors who helped me make this a better book and for always being constructive, even when they could have been critical.

A huge thank-you to my fab agent and friend Charlotte Robertson – for all the talks and support and general loveliness, and whose help throughout made writing this book not only possible but a genuinely enjoyable experience.

A very special thank-you to my absolutely wonderful parents, whose wisdom and persepectives on life and living still resonate with me every day. And a massive thank-you to the other two musketeers in my life, my Teddy and my Jessie – you were both so cool about me working late when I needed to and also about stopping me working late when you knew I needed to ... thank you for the balance, the perspective and for making life so much fun.

And finally, to my great friend Angus, neither a twenty-something nor a girl but a great one for challenging me and asking awkward questions, a huge thank-you for sending me reams of great articles that 'I absolutley had to read' and for being such an amazing friend. Angus, you are definitely my honorary power girl.

Introduction

Dear twenty-something

Being in your twenties will be in equal measure exhilarating and daunting, liberating and constraining, effortless and complicated. It is the period in your life when every headline and every tag line in ads, movies or songs, overt or implied, is telling you that you should be 'having the time of your life'. And while I'm sure that sometimes it will feel that way, no doubt there will be others when you'll feel overwhelmed, uncertain and maybe even a little scared about the future. And that's the thing about this awesome decade in your life – that, on the one hand, it's about letting go, making mistakes and having fun, while, on the other, it's about getting your life on track and figuring out who you are and what you want to do. But don't worry, these things are not incongruent; in fact, you need to let go and make mistakes if you are to stand any chance of knowing what you want out of life – or at least, what you don't.

So these years can be a time of genuine self-discovery, but they can also be a time of feeling pressure from society, peers and parents to live up to certain expectations. It may feel really important to you that the world perceives you and the decisions you make in the 'right' way; that's probably why social networking is so prevalent in our psyches – because it allows us to quantify how well we are doing by providing us with up-to-the-minute assessments of what people 'like' about us.

The thing is, though, editing your life so that it appears OK to others is a sure-fire way to feel unfulfilled and unhappy. Stop engaging with yourself in terms of how other people see you and focus on what really matters to you. Don't seek validation through what others 'like' about your life – instead, figure out what *you* like by getting out, experiencing life and making genuine connections with people. In real life there are successes and failures, good days and hard days, and one of the most significant lessons I learned in my twenties was to allow myself to experience both, without apologising or even seeking praise. *Your* experience of what is going on in *your* life is what ultimately counts.

Now, as appealing as it is to make a checklist of everything that you need to get sorted by your thirtieth birthday, remember that sometimes things will happen that you don't expect, and no matter how organised you are or how much planning you do, you will be blindsided by stuff that life throws at you. Because of this, adaptability, more than anything, is the trait that will get you not only through your twenties, but through life. By this I mean being able to react to what is actually happening, rather than trying to force-fit your life into some predetermined idea of what you think it ought to look like.

Friends – real friends – and family are amazing resources, so develop and nurture these relationships. And while you may feel that only your peers can really understand you, believe me, the insights you will get from hanging out with people who are older than you and who see things from a different perspective are a vital part of making sense not only of your past, but also your future. People who have been here longer will challenge you to view things from a different angle, so make time for your favourite aunt or grandma; she may have a view on things that might surprise you.

Your generation, I think more than any other, is plagued by the need to be perfect – and if this is your mission, let me spoil the suspense: you are not perfect; none of us is. You *will* make mistakes and you *will* feel like dropping out of things that you aren't that good at. But the thing is, you can't just drop out of life, so making peace with the idea that you can actually enjoy and learn from something without having to be the best at it is important. Allow yourself to make mistakes; believe me, the insight that you glean from getting things wrong is really valuable, and playing it safe by not taking chances is a far riskier strategy than just going for it, even if you aren't certain of the outcome. But don't forget that although going for it and working hard are great, you still need balance – burnout is not a badge of honour. So while engaging in competitive sleep deprivation with your colleagues to prove that you can work harder than anyone else might be tempting, it will, eventually, catch up with you. Your health is something you should never take for granted, at any age, so remember the basics: eat well, ditching the processed stuff and fad diets; sleep well – research shows that most of us really do need seven to eight hours to function optimally; and stay fit – exercise is a great stress-buster, as well as being good for your physical health, so make it part of your self-care routine.

And know how lucky you are. One of the most exciting things about being a young adult today is how easily you can impact the world around you. You can literally be the change you want to see, so take advantage of that. The amazing positive side of technology and connectivity is that social movements are gaining momentum quicker and are more powerful than ever before. You have a voice. Whether it's democratic uprisings, social-equality campaigns or e-petitions that change laws and affect government policy, you have the tools to make a difference. Your generation can make its collective voice heard louder than any other's in modern history. You are super lucky because you don't have many of the ideological constraints of linear social and political structures that your parents grew up with. Over the past few years we have seen the calling to account of government, journalism and the banks – all have been questioned and challenged, and I think there is a growing sense that things don't have to be the way they are just because that's the way they've always been. For these reasons, and despite all the difficulties you may face, I think we're going to see some amazing things from your generation.

Already, we're seeing a fourth generation of feminism, and this time it's a humanist feminism – so it's not about exchanging patriarchy with matriarchy, but saying that if you really want equality, it needs to come from both directions. I think slowly we may even begin to see a redefinition of success. I've heard from a lot of young women in their twenties who have told me that they are questioning much of the pathological materialism that's been in play for so long, so maybe there will be a backlash about the definitions of success; maybe there will be a re-emphasis on community, on connection and on happiness. And that is so cool. Because in life, an attitude of *How can I contribute?* rather than *What can I get out of this?* not only boosts our happiness as individuals, but also generates genuine positive change in the world.

So, you fab twenty-something, enjoy and savour this decade. Yes, there is a lot to get done, but remember: figuring out what you want to do with your life is, in most cases, an ongoing process; it's not one eureka moment that hits you out of the blue. You will grow as a character and, as you do, you will learn and figure out what you want. Be open to experiences; live your life according to your values; follow your own path and be kind to others – and to yourself; and this is key: beware of negative, defeatist self-talk. You can't control what happens to you in life, but, crucially, you can always control how you react to it. Life is a product of your decisions, and your ability to make good ones is ruled by your beliefs and the way that you think about yourself and the world around you.

As the famous saying goes: 'Whether you think you can or you think you can't, you're right.' And just for the record, I have no doubt that you can.

Love
Dr Linda

CHAPTER 1

•

Perfect Lives

'I hate letting people down, but more than that, I don't want to let myself down. I know that I can be anything and do anything, and I look around and there are all these really successful people living these "perfect" lives and I want that to be me. It's just that sometimes I feel that no matter how hard I try I can't manage to keep up – maybe I just need to try harder.'

Sarah, aged twenty-five

So this is what I think happened: as our world became more visual, we felt a need to ensure that those images of ourselves that were seen and analysed by everyone around us were as pristine and as beautiful as possible. In fact, precisely because our world became so visual, we began to look at ourselves a lot more, focusing on the details, thinking about how we might look to others and, eventually, perceiving and relating to ourselves in the third person. This meant that our perception was influenced less by what we saw in the mirror and more by what we thought others would see when they looked at us.

From Airbrushed Photos to Airbrushed Lives

Over time, we realised that these pictures were no longer just about the way we looked, but that they were messages to others about who we were and the lives we led. So we needed to create the perfect picture – we needed to be the girl everyone was telling us we should be. And when our pictures didn't come out the way we wanted them to, we fixed them – we edited and we Photoshopped. And then, at some point, we decided that if we could Photoshop our pics, then maybe we could Photoshop our lives, too. We could try and make our lives look perfect – and what does a perfect life look like? Well, perfect is the girl that has it all, of course ...

Whether it's the proliferation or the homogeneous nature of the images of beauty and success that wallpaper our world, we know what a beautiful woman looks like – and we know what a perfect life looks like, too. We live in a world that floods us with expectations about everything – from what we should weigh to what we should wear to how often we should be having sex and how much money we should be making. As a consequence, we begin to feel that we need to tick all these boxes in order to have the 'Perfect Life'. When we inevitably fall short, we feel anxious – we feel that we are failing and have the sense that we are losing control.

The worrying thing is that this sense of not achieving

enough or living up to our potential seems to kick in earlier and earlier. Both in my work as an academic and in my private practice I see young women in their twenties and early thirties who so often feel a genuine sense of anxiety and unease about not doing enough, accomplishing enough – about not being perfect. Of course, it's important to have goals and role models to help us achieve our aims in life; however, society's ideals – whether the ultimate job, look or quinoa recipe – are general, whereas our individual needs are, of necessity, specific. So as soon as we allow these arbitrary ideals and expectations to become our sole focus and the standard by which we measure ourselves, we not only limit our freedom to choose who we want to be but, more damagingly, we judge ourselves negatively when we don't meet them. Then nothing but the best is good enough and, all of a sudden, even the best is not good enough either: that speech where we received a standing ovation could have been improved; that soufflé could have tasted so much better with just three more minutes in the oven; and if only we'd tweaked the font on that PowerPoint presentation, it would have looked perfect. We become so focused on the 'ideal' that we forget, ignore and, eventually, simply stop being able to see our own needs.

Feminism is Not Anti-feminist

If we are going to try to figure out why by the time we enter our twenties we are already feeling the stress and anxiety of having it all, then I think we need to start with a brief history of feminism. After all, feminism has historically shaped society's views about equality and informed our choices as well as our beliefs regarding success and, to some extent, what a complete, happy woman should look like.

For the record, I am a feminist. I know the word is loaded with value judgements, tainted with political and social ideology and, ironically, used as a weapon by and against women to make them feel they don't know what is best for them. To me, feminism is about equality; it's not a movement designed to replace patriarchy with matriarchy. And the reason why I am a feminist is simple: I don't believe that a person's gender should determine their humanity. That, and the fact that even though Elizabeth Blackwell graduated from medical school in 1849, the following riddle still stumps people today, getting on for two centuries later:

A father and his son are in a car accident. The father dies at the scene and the son is rushed to the hospital. At the hospital the surgeon looks at the boy and says, 'I can't operate on this boy, he is my son.' How can this be?

Feminism can be divided broadly into two areas: equity feminism and gender feminism. The first wave of feminism, which started in the late nineteenth century, was about equality; so it focused on overturning legal inequalities that got in the way of civic rights and included things like the right to equal pay, women's right to have a say with regard to their children, the right to own and inherit property and equal employment opportunities, as well, of course, as the right to vote. It also sought to maintain the value of housewives.

Beginning around the time of the social revolution of the 1960s, the second wave of feminism had more to do with gender equality. It broadened the debate to address gender norms and the role of women in society. Campaigners fought to provide women with all the same opportunities as men and highlighted issues around affirmative action, rape, domestic violence, pornography, sexism in the media and reproductive choice. The latter included a fight for information about and access to birth control, as well as the decriminalisation of abortion; progress in this regard meant that for the first time the ideals of equal opportunity could actually work in practice.

As the women's movement gained momentum and more women went to law school, feminist critiques of the law began to emerge. A common criticism that came up during this period centred round the way history was written. Feminists highlighted the fact that traditional historians wrote solely from the male perspective, without reference to women's roles and contributions in structuring society, the point being that this created a bias regarding political concepts, gender values, social arrangements and even human nature.

By way of addressing this, some second-wave feminists sought equality through challenging and, in certain cases, the removal of distinctions between masculinity and femininity. This had an impact; consequently, there was a move towards women mirroring the promiscuity that was accepted for males in society. At the same time, there was increased pressure to view many traditional female roles, such as motherhood, as signs of conforming to a patriarchal society.

Although great advancements happened during this period a lot of the pressures that we still contend with today started to emerge. The feminist tag line of the day changed from 'Women are entitled to equal opportunities' to 'Women can do it all'. Then the word 'can' somehow morphed into 'should' – perhaps in order to prove that we were, in fact, equal, worthy and good enough.

Third-wave feminism began in the early 1990s and addressed the fact that many women felt that the values and ideals expounded by second-wave feminists had become too limiting. Women began to rebel against earlier definitions of femininity that they saw as restricting individual freedom. It is viewed as an all-encompassing wave of feminism, taking in gender, racial, economic and social justice.

Some people believe we are now entering a fourth wave of feminism in an attempt to revive the principles of the first wave within the context and complexity of twenty-first-century life. There is a move towards addressing themes like spirituality, as well as lifting standards for both sexes. The fourth wave is intended to 'help women find *their* feminism' and allow them to enjoy what feels good to them, from fashion to sex, without fear of being ejected from feminist ranks.

So over the past few decades we have been developing the skills that should have allowed us to finally gain the social and political equity we fought for with such fervour. However, despite the progress we've made (and we have made a lot), the truth is that it still doesn't translate into parity on the home front or power at the top. We work for major corporations, but rarely lead them: as of 2012, we account for only 16 per cent of partners in the largest law firms and just 15 per cent of senior executives in Fortune 500 firms. We run for political office, but still secure nowhere near the number of seats held by men (pre-election pledges in the UK that one-third of ministerial jobs would be taken by women before 2015 don't seem to have come true, although currently one in five MPs is female; while in the US there have been just thirty-nine female senators in the nation's history and twenty of these are currently serving). Even in Hollywood, where women are much more visible, they make up only 7 per cent of directors and it took the Academy Award jury until 2010 to give a female director an Oscar in recognition of her work. Oh ... and we still earn around 15 per cent less than men per hour in the UK[1] and, on average, only seventy-seven cents to every man's dollar in the US, according to data released in 2013 by the US Census Bureau.[2]

So while we've achieved a lot, clearly, there is still plenty to do. But although it's really important to get the numbers right and bring balance to the gender equation, it's just as important to pay attention to the pressure that has accompanied the changes we've experienced over the years and consider how these calls to action are affecting us on an individual basis.

The irony is that feminism was supposed to eliminate restrictive notions of womanhood – the pressure to compare, compete and to have it all. It was meant to challenge and change traditionally limiting ideas of how women were expected to behave and who they were supposed to be. However, I think we may have misconstrued the messages behind the theorising and somehow got to a point where instead of focusing on equality and progress we began to view certain feminist principles as a means to becoming perfect people. After all, if it's the case that we *can* do *anything*, maybe we should do *everything*. So perhaps it's time to reformulate feminism; perhaps what's needed is a move to more authenticity when it comes to describing the experience of being a woman – more honesty, but certainly no more pressure. We need to figure out which aspects of ourselves – of our womanhood – feel better in practice rather than in theory.

Effortless

> *'Girls need to have all their grandmothers wanted them to have, while looking as pretty as their mothers wanted them to look . . . You try so hard to be who everyone wants you to be while attempting to maintain some kind of individuality and in the end you seem to lose everything.'*

Debora L. Spar[3]

In the same way that we are clear about what beauty looks like, we also know what happiness and success are supposed to look like. And they look effortless. The women who seem to juggle work and family – effortless; the supermodel tweeting pictures of herself cramming Big Macs in her mouth, while maintaining a 22-inch waist – effortless; the accidental dot-com millionaire who wrote an idea on the back of a beer mat and sold off a multi-million-dollar company a year later – effortless. We are bombarded with so many fairy-tale-ending success stories that we see these not only as the norm, but expected. And the fact that our sound-bite society distils everything down to the simplest formula, i.e. success = wanting it enough, doesn't help either. So we skim over the hard work, the trials, the sacrifices and the failures of successful people; in fact, we don't really even engage with the notion that for every success story there are millions of people who don't have autobiography-worthy lives, and assume that everyone but us is 'living their best lives' and 'being their best selves'.

Our view of success is skewed – in terms of both what it is and how to achieve it. We imagine that being a successful woman today means being too cool and confident to worry about pressures and expectations. But we *do* worry – in fact, we worry about more or less everything. A study that tracked couples over three months found that men, on average, worry about three things every day, but women worry about twelve. No surprise, therefore, that women are more vulnerable to anxiety disorders. In fact, chronic anxiety is a cause of depression. This goes some way to explaining why women are twice as likely as men to be diagnosed with clinical depression, although, of course, it also has to do with the fact that we are more willing to discuss these issues with health professionals.

Several studies attest to our need to assert control over our lives via worrying. In a 2011 survey, 22 per cent of women said they felt worried, nervous or anxious daily or weekly, compared to 16 per cent of men.[4] Another study reported that more women (27 per cent) than men (20 per cent) worry about the health of a partner or child and more women (25 per cent) than men (15 per cent) say children are a very significant source of stress in their lives.[5] According to the website LiveScience, a Polaris poll in 2012 found that 'men were more likely to say work issues were causing them angst, while women were significantly more likely to cite financial issues, lack of time, family problems, living situation and relationship issues'. The poll illustrates an old stereotype and could have been called 'Men Stressed by Work, Women Stressed by Work AND Everything Else'.

Worse still, we have come to believe that we need to be great at everything simultaneously – and preferably without any help. You don't need to be an expert to figure out that a person (female or male) cannot sustain a sixty-hour working week and still have the same time and energy to invest in other aspects of their life. Yet women sit across from me in my clinics almost every day berating themselves for failing to balance and to achieve perfection.

So instead of celebrating the feminist gains made since all those suffragettes marched from Hyde Park to Exeter Hall back in 1907, it seems we are now in a position where we're faced with impossible expectations. We still have the old-fashioned pressures of being perfect girlfriends and wives, as well as the more modern-day demands that we be physically beautiful, ageless and sexy, have brilliant entrepreneurial minds and be creative and ambitious. The result? We are always feeling anxious that we are not doing or being enough and we constantly feel less than perfect and guilty for not being able to have it all.

Not so effortless after all, then.

Having It All

Earlier this year Yahoo! CEO Marissa Mayer riled many working mothers with her decision to ban employees from working at home and her claim that having a baby was 'way easier' than she thought. Some labelled Mayer's comments as 'retro and politically incorrect',[6] but the main criticism was that she was perpetuating the outdated (or at least what we hoped was slowly starting to become outdated) notion that women 'can have it all'. But here's the thing: no one can have it all – not even Marissa Mayer. Because the fact is that we are socialised differently from men. For example, when a woman drops her kids off at nursery school she feels guilty for leaving them, but when her husband drops them off he feels good about it because he is being an active parent. Women are socialised into the expectation that childcare is their responsibility, regardless of whether or not they work the same hours as their partner.

So maybe we need to think about what 'having it all' actually means. Come to think of it, why aren't more books, polls and researchers asking if *men* can have it all? Why are we so fixated on the juggling abilities of the Marissa Mayers of this world and not asking how Richard Branson's or

Warren Buffett's running of their multinational companies and investments is impacting on their parenting skills and home lives? As Gloria Steinem famously said, 'I have yet to hear a man ask for advice on how to combine marriage and a career.' The fact is that we derive our idea of what we want by internalising the messages – both covert and overt – from the world around us. So yes, the fact that there are more polls about women juggling home and life matters; the assumption is that this is a women's issue that needs to be sorted out by women, yet it affects all of us, men and women alike – and not just at home but in the workplace, too. But we don't talk about that enough.

In any case, it's not just getting the work–life balance right that is supposed to make us better and happier – it's about doing as much as possible, and the problem with that is time, because no matter how rich or successful we are, we all have a finite number of hours in the day in which we need to prioritise all the things we need to do to keep life running smoothly. So maybe we need to stop asking whether or not women can have it all and start asking instead: 'What's important to me right now at this time in my life?' And the question is as much one of values as it is of gender roles.

What complicates things is that we are socialised into believing what 'should be' of value to our gender. We need to look amazing like Kate Moss, have a career like Hillary, cook like Nigella, dance like Rihanna and get back into our skinny jeans as soon as our Caesarean stitches are healed. And we need to do it all without breaking a sweat. That's the biggest lie of all. We feel guilty about not being perfect because we are lying to each other, making perfect look effortless.

Sustain the Sisterhood

So we judge ourselves harshly, but we also judge each other – and the effects of these judgements can be really damaging. A cursory look at recent news stories brings up lots of examples: poor Condoleezza Rice, so successful but left without a boyfriend; poor Jen Aniston, great career, but still no baby; arrogant Sheryl Sandberg, she doesn't really want to help other women, she just wants to advance her own brand. Oh well, they paid for their success – they can't do it all ... It seems the way that we relate to each other as women is taking an ominous turn. We've gone from deriding men for their patriarchal oppression and its effect on our happiness (see Germaine Greer) to belittling and deriding ourselves and our imperfect bodies (see Naomi Wolf) and we're now at a point where, worryingly, it seems that to feel good about ourselves, we need to judge and belittle the choices of other women. Perhaps we need to start defining ourselves not in terms of opposition – 'I don't think strong women should care about their looks'; 'I'm not the kind of woman who wears pink'; 'I'm not the kind of woman who's into playing the happy homemaker' – but rather by what we *are*, leaving room for the notion that we don't all have to agree on what a well-balanced, happy woman should be like.

While there is no doubt that we have choices today that our mothers never had, it is the freedom to be who we want to be and the ability to recognise what we care about and want the most that should dictate the choices that we make. Defining ourselves by what we love, not what we hate, and being pro, not just anti, is a good start.

It's been more than five decades since women rocked the world with the feminist and sexual revolutions. The whole point of these was to bring us together, to take us out of isolation and into communities that sought the achievement of a fairer society. But sadly, instead of being enriched and strengthened by these cries of sisterhood, instead of gaining that sense of entitlement that we fought for, we are, in many ways, stuck in a purgatory of perfection. We are trying so hard to do so much and do it so perfectly that we are setting ourselves up for failure, along with the feelings of guilt and anxiety that go hand in hand with the sense of letting ourselves and everyone else down.

Perfectionism and the Fear of Failure

Perfectionism is more than just a need to do things to the best of our ability – it's a state of mind characterised by polarised thinking that makes us feel there is nothing between the extremes of absolutely perfect and dreadfully awful. More than that, it makes us focus on the outcomes of our actions, so we are constantly assessing ourselves to see if we are measuring up – and underlying this, unsurprisingly, is a fear of failure. And it's not just about getting perfect grades or sculpting perfect abs or executing the perfect chocolate soufflé for a dinner party – it's also about doing as much as possible and as well as possible in order to appear 'well rounded' or, better yet, like the girl who can do it all.

From a psychological point of view, the need to appear perfect stems from the belief that being perfect will somehow protect us. It is based on the notion that if we look, behave and perform perfectly, we can avoid the pain of judgement and blame. Of course, with the need to be perfect or do it all comes the concomitant fear of what happens if we fail, let people down or simply aren't good enough.

It's really important to note that unlike the attempt to do your best, which is actually a relatively healthy way to approach goals, perfectionism isn't a viable goal, strategy or ambition. Rather, it's an unhealthy defence mechanism that leads to burnout and serves to hinder rather than protect us: if we perform well, we won't have to deal with the shame or blame or anxiety that go along with letting people down. Perfectionism takes the enjoyment out of experiences and focuses us on the outcome of our actions to the point that we are never fully engaged in what we do. Worst of all, because there is no such thing as perfect we are left feeling perpetually dissatisfied.

To complicate things further, for something to be perfect, someone else has to deem it so, therefore there is the constant sense of being judged; and because it can be difficult to separate what we do from who we are, perfectionists can feel that when people are judging their work, they're actually judging them and their worth as a person. And that is when perfectionism becomes particularly problematic – when it begins to be linked with self-worth. When the way we value ourselves is dependent on achieving perfection or the validation that we get from it, we invariably seek it out as a means to feel not perfect, but just OK with who we are. Put simply, seeking perfection is probably the best way to feel bad about yourself.

Research suggests that girls who are perfectionists are more likely to suffer from obsessive-compulsive disorder (OCD), depression and eating disorders.[7] In a society that floods us with unattainable expectations around every topic imaginable, putting down the perfection shield is scary. But whether it's an essay for uni, trying to secure the ideal job, following the perfect diet, finding Mr Right or choosing the 'it' bag of the season – it isn't real. And maybe our pursuit of all this is a part of what is holding us back.

The quest to be perfect can make us less efficient because we're more likely to linger and find new things to improve on. It can make us less effective, so we focus on details, without consciously considering whether they're really necessary. But worst of all, a desire to be perfect over-complicates what we are trying to achieve to the extent that it becomes subconsciously intimidating. We anticipate problems that may never arise, focusing on what could go wrong, rather than what will probably go OK.

So perhaps the dearth of female CEOs and Fortune 500 industry leaders also has something to do with our fear of not being good enough, of letting others down. If we are making decisions out of worry and fear, then it's no wonder that we stop 'leaning in', as Sheryl Sandberg suggests, when it comes to business – the anxiety of not living up to expectations can be crippling, and if we expect only perfection from ourselves before we can make a move, we are not going to see the level and speed of change and equality in the business world that we'd like to.

Instead of trying to achieve perfection, perhaps we should figure out not just *what* we want, but *why* we want it. When did we decide that we needed it and for what purpose? Does it fit into the notion of the women we think we *should* be or the women we really *want* to be? We need to ask ourselves why we are so paralysed by what other people think.

There is a therapeutic model known as Person Centred Therapy which has at its core something called 'unconditional positive regard'. It is based on the idea that if you can foster a therapeutic relationship with a person where he or she believes that they are valued and respected for who they are, regardless of achievements and failures, then they will begin to heal and grow emotionally. We all want to feel worthy of love and respect and acceptance. But we need to be able to give these things to ourselves without prerequisites. So no more saying, 'I'll be worthy when I lose 20 pounds/get a corner office/find a boyfriend/gain my parents' approval – when I can do it all and look like I'm not even trying.' We just need to feel worthy *now*, as we are.

It's not easy to find the courage to move from 'What will people think?' to 'I am enough', but think of it like this: is it scarier ignoring what other people think or ignoring how you feel, what you believe in and, ultimately, who you are?

How Do You Do It?

One of the questions that I get asked a lot is 'How do you do it all?' I have to say it always stumps me because a) I genuinely don't think that doing it all is actually doable and b) I don't ever set out to do it *all*. I set out to do what is most important to me – and sometimes it works and sometimes – well, it doesn't.

Early on in my career, even though I was head of a university post-graduate department, I was often mistaken for a research assistant or administrator. One time, at a big heads-of-department meeting, I was even asked condescendingly by a colleague to 'please organise the coffee, dear'. Interestingly, I don't think that was just about the fact that I was a young course director because standing next to me was a male friend, the same age as me and also a lecturer, who never seemed to have that problem. The idea that I didn't look the part bothered me. I did a lot of soul searching, wondering if I should change my hair or dress differently. I felt I had to work harder, publish more, lecture better and be in every way possible more ambitious and more productive to be seen as a serious academic. And while all in all it worked and I advanced quickly in my career, I still felt that I wasn't allowed to drop a ball or be anything but 'perfect' – because if I did, I would probably confirm people's belief that really I didn't have what it took. Over the years that is something that I have worked on: I decided that rather than conforming to some socks-and-sandals stereotype of what an academic should look like, I would invest my energy instead in being myself and focusing on my work. By being true to the things that were important to me I was able to develop my own niche in my field. I gave myself permission to be different, to take risks and, most importantly, to make mistakes. I accepted that, actually, perfect was not really an option. I think that's why to this day I love my work.

Regardless of how much I love my work though, like most women, I juggle: I have sneaked out of meetings to watch my daughter Jessie play netball and, conversely, have missed her piano recitals when I had a deadline looming. I have sprinted through airports and train stations to make it home earlier in order to have dinner with my family. And when Jessie was a baby the desire to be the perfect mother and make sure I was always around meant I would take her with me everywhere: so she would sit playing quietly in the corner on her activity mat while I had meetings with my doctoral students, discussing the virtues of quantitative versus qualitative data analysis; she and my mum would fly with me to the States when I had to work on projects out there; and she has been into practically every TV green room in London, waiting for me to give my 'expert analysis' on whatever current affairs story I happened to be commenting on. Once, in my attempt to 'do it all', I accidentally locked her in the car as I hurried to get to a book signing. I then had to get the (very judgemental) security guard to help me break a window to get her out. (Thankfully, she slept through the whole ordeal, so hopefully any memories of me panicking and screaming frantically won't have registered!)

I have felt the pressure of having to look better, work harder, cook more healthily and generally do more. But I have learned this: I can't work sixty-hour weeks and still go to every school event; I can't look polished and immaculate all the time; and without the help of my amazing husband and my lovely parents, who fly over from Cyprus whenever I need them, I can't be the mum I want to be either.

So Now What?

To make any real progress in moving forward we need to deconstruct the myth that perfection does, or indeed ever will, exist.

The unrealistic expectations we have of ourselves and our 'role' in society come from many disparate areas – from media and advertising messages to biology and socio-political history. Many women hold that we need to continue fighting overt discrimination and campaign for change at government level, so we can secure better day-care facilities, more flexitime at work and co-parenting at home. But while there is undoubtedly value in this approach, I don't think it goes far enough in addressing the underlying cause of the problem – because the issues go beyond money or policy alone.

What we need is an attitudinal shift. And the first thing we have to do is to start talking, not just to each other, but to the men in our lives as well. Women are often scared of raising the topic of gender with men, thinking they'll be seen as difficult; at the same time, men who may be inclined to want to help are often afraid to say or do something that may be labelled as politically incorrect. So we end up with a situation where productive discussions that could actually make a difference are simply not taking place.

Next, we need to acknowledge that biology matters. It doesn't have to determine your entire life, but simply stated, the fact that women experience pregnancy for nine months, then childbirth and the need to physically and emotionally sustain a baby for the first critical moths of life should be taken into account. And while companies can help with fair maternity-leave periods and family-friendly workplaces, the unadorned truth is that women who have children and go to work will always need to make choices that most men won't. So take it as a given that at some point you will have to make these decisions and think things through in terms of what will help you in your particular case: think about when to have a baby and where you'll live, in terms of proximity to both work and extended family that might be able to help support you with childcare. The point is to make conscious choices, even if they aren't easy, rather than try to do it all.

And really importantly, I don't think we should be afraid of acknowledging that men and women differ. Generally speaking, a review of gender studies research indicates that we are less comfortable with big risks, we may be less directly confrontational and less likely to speak of our successes. We are also more likely to favour personal relationships over hierarchical ones, are better at talking about our feelings and worse at reading maps. So what? Instead of pretending that these differences don't exist, let's begin having discussions about them – let's understand and analyse them and construct a society that sees value in diversity and, better yet, one that is directed by the passions, skills and interests not just of men, but of women as well. Feminism was supposed to give us the freedom and power to live in a fair world and to shape our lives in any way we see fit. But with more choices today than women have ever had before, we need to be careful that we don't become slaves to those choices. We need to choose wisely, and we need to stop striving for mythical concepts like 'having it all' and being 'perfect' because, ultimately, they are as disingenuous and potentially damaging as the idea of 'happy ever after'. Female empowerment should not be a rejection of who we really are or what we really want; instead, it should give us a sense of entitlement to write our own scripts, rather than having them handed to us by the media, by tradition, by history or by commercialisation.

We also need to stop thinking that success is effortless. When we worry, we feel we are somehow deficient *because we worry*; but the truth is, we all do it: we worry about how we measure up, if we are being good enough friends or lovers, if we are eating right, saving enough, travelling to the right destinations. We worry. So it's vital that we acknowledge that it isn't easy and, as such, that we should stop pretending otherwise.

This doesn't mean you should stop going for your dream job or 2.1 kids or anything that you aspire to. Ambition is wonderful and important and you should strive and fight and work hard for all that you want. But don't fall into the trap of thinking you have failed if you're not a CEO by the time you're thirty or, indeed, if you don't actually want to be a CEO and want to stay at home and be a mum.

Remember – it's about striving for what *you* want, not what you think you should have. And if you find yourself looking around at other women and wondering how they manage life's balancing act so well, take it from someone who often gets mistaken for 'having it all' – we all make trade-offs, and as long as those trade-offs make sense in relation to you and your values right now (because these may change over time), then that's OK.

•

CHAPTER 2

Hot Enough?

'It's always there, no matter how much you achieve, or how well you do at something, you sort of suspect that still, what really matters is how pretty or thin you are . . .'

Camilla, aged twenty-six

My little girl Jessie was born in late 2002. At the time I was doing a lot of research and clinical work in the area of body image (BI) and becoming even more aware than I had been during my training of how our desire for physical perfection was entering young women's psyche in a dangerous way. As a consequence, I began to write *Mirror Mirror*, my first book in the area. I wrote it for Jessie: as I gazed at my perfect little baby I couldn't bear to imagine that one day she might look in the mirror and despise the reflection she saw there – something that I see almost daily with the women and girls I work with in my clinic. Looking back on that book now, a lot remains the same: BI is still 'a person's thoughts, perception and feelings about their body';

body preoccupation still leads to general life dissatisfaction and the values of popular society still underscore the way that women perceive and value their bodies.

But there are differences, too. Technological advancements and the marrying of media and celebrity culture mean that not only are we seeing more pictures of perfection everywhere, but we are producing more pictures of ourselves than ever before. As a consequence, we are both subconsciously buying into idealised notions of beauty and perfection while consciously attempting to replicate them, in most cases unsuccessfully, so we're always left feeling 'less than'.

What I think is fundamental to understand about body image is that it goes deeper than merely the way we perceive our physical attributes. It is the mental image we hold of ourselves; it is that image that we use to think about who we are. As such, it has the capacity to influence our self-esteem, to affect decision-making and dictate our beliefs about not only who we are, but how we fit into the world and what we should expect from it.

Our preoccupation with all things physical combined with the demedicalisation of cosmetic surgery and the idea that being thin is somehow a reflection of personal virtue has turned us into a generation of self-obsessed, appearance junkies. We contemplate, discuss and strategise about our appearance with the vigour once reserved for high-level chess masters. And the thing is, the more preoccupied we are with our appearance, the more likely we are to begin to self-objectify; that is, to relate to ourselves in the third person. So we're never really looking at a reflection of who we are, but rather we are constantly assessing what we look like to others. The American Psychological Association has described this kind of self-objectification as a national epidemic[1] and it's no different on this side of the pond. When I did a review for the UK government on sexualisation of young people, self-objectification was a core theme that arose time and time again.[2]

Self-objectification not only involves looking at yourself from the point of view of an observer, thus ignoring any intrinsic traits that make you you, it also means that you are more likely to chronically monitor your physical appearance to the detriment of whatever else you could be engaging with. A study that set out to examine whether women who are more aware of their bodies from within are less likely to think of their bodies as objects yielded some interesting results.[3] The researchers asked nineteen- to twenty-six-year-old healthy female volunteers to 'listen to their bodies' by focusing on and counting their heartbeat. Their accuracy in this 'heartbeat task' was compared with their degree of self-objectification, the results showing that the more accurate they were at detecting their heartbeats, the less likely they were to think of their bodies as objects.

These findings are really important because they underscore the idea that constantly relating to ourselves in the third person actually makes us less aware of our bodies and their functionality. It gives credence to the notion that by self-objectifying, women are more likely to devalue their physical competence and even their health.

Just think about how much this reduces our ability to engage with life in a healthy way. Imagine you are walking on the beach enjoying the last day of your holiday. If you are self-objectifying, you are likely to be so focused on the visual impact you are having on others' consciousness – adjusting your hair, your sarong, etc. – that you won't enjoy the feel of the sun on your shoulders or the sand between your toes. This minimises your ability to focus on your experience, so that you are no longer engaging with what you are doing and are instead constantly assessing how you appear to others – your experience is no longer your own, but rather is beholden to your beliefs about other people's beliefs about you! Think about what this means in terms of your ability to make the most of your life.

In the 2011 documentary *Miss Representation* (which I think should be mandatory viewing for anyone trying to understand the role of the media in how women see themselves) the point is made that women who self-objectify are more likely to be depressed, have eating disorders, lower grades, reduced confidence and ambition and even a decline in cognitive function. These insights, substantiated by several studies,[4] are genuinely worrying. Think about what they mean in terms of equality, in society, in the workplace and at home – even in terms of the sense of volition we have over the way our world is run: with higher self-objectification comes lower political efficacy, so we could potentially have a whole generation of women who are less likely to run for political office or even vote!

The impact of this phenomenon and the harm that it can do was captured beautifully in 1977 by the French philosopher, Michel Foucault:

There is no need for arms, physical violence,
material constraints. Just a gaze. An inspecting
gaze, a gaze which each individual under its weight
will end by [internalizing] to the point that [she] is
[her] own overseer, each individual thus exercising
surveillance over, and against [her]self.[5]

Self-objectification has the potential to hinder women's progress in so many fundamental ways. We can do better – so much better – than merely look good and until we get that, we will continue to compromise not only our mental and physical wellbeing, but the fundamental human right to imperfection.

The Skinny Contest

What our peers think of us becomes really important in our early teens and never really lets up completely thereafter. We look to each other for guidance on what is important – what we should be thinking or doing – and we draw comparisons with others to gauge our performance. According to Social Comparison Theory, the reason why we evaluate ourselves against other people and social standards in general is because most of the opinions and attitudes we come across cannot really be evaluated objectively. So looking to our peers and social norms is the next best thing.

Now think about how our world is structured – gone are the days when we had extended families and were in contact with several generations, so we could benefit from the

wisdom of a great-aunt or grandmother. Today's age strati-
fication means that from the time we reach adolescence we
are all herded together with people of the same age, with the
same concerns and insecurities, to the extent that some theorists believe that colleges and universities have become
'incubators for eating disorders'.[6] Central to this theory is
the fact that the norms of the groups you are living with
become inescapable – you eat together, live together, work
out and party together. And these norms are particularly
influential at times when you are experiencing anything
new – you want to fit in, so you look around at what is
normal and try to emulate it. But at some point these comparisons turn into competition and that is when things get
problematic.

According to researchers, misperceptions about how we
measure up accelerate over time. So, for example, while initially you may think that you and your peers are around the
same weight, one year on you assume that others are losing
weight while you are gaining,[7] so you begin to diet in order
to feel in control, and this often escalates, so that eventually
it's not you controlling your eating habits, but rather, it's
your eating habits controlling you.

Another theory that is often put forward is that of the
Superwoman syndrome: in a culture where there is so much
pressure to succeed and appear perfect, the stress starts early
on and is punctuated by the 'fat fear' that both covertly and
overtly underlies how we feel about ourselves.[8] Our bodies
and our appearance become hangers on which to hang our
insecurities. When we feel out of control – when we feel we
can no longer be the best student, employee, partner or

mother – we decide that at least we can be the best at controlling our looks or appetite.

Then there is also the evolutionary issue, whereby, at the basest level, we all need to ensure our genetic survival and so we feel we are competing for mates; and with the central message being that thin and beautiful is what matters and what is desirable, the equation goes something like this:

I need to be perfect to be accepted
+
I'm in competition with all these other girls for men
+
Being thin means I'm pretty and in control and
    desirable
= I will win the contest by being the thinnest I
    can be.

So we end up seeing body-image issues and eating disorders being played out in terms of sexual competition. According to evolutionary psychologist Geoffrey Miller, schools and colleges become so racially and socially homogeneous that young people need to find ways to outdo each other.[9] Add to that the fact that more young women are not only going on to further education, but are also getting postgrad' degrees and this kind of age-group ghettoisation is lasting a lot longer than it used to. And a minimised engagement with a more heterogeneous outside environment means that the focus on the self becomes more intense.

Young or old, the ability to assess oneself and one's life independent of peer pressure is important. We already live in a society that values the body over the mind, and if we don't challenge this idea, then we face reaching the point where our bodies will define our identity, rather than just being a part of it.

Body Image and the Media

The core message of most of today's media goes something like this: 'If you are skinny and pretty, then you will have a happy, fulfilled life. If you are overweight, deemed unattractive or showing signs of ageing, well, then you don't really deserve to expect too much out of life; after all, your worth as a woman really lies in how attractive you are to those around you.'

It is frightening how little emphasis today is placed on the emotional and intellectual aspects of who we are – that while we are inundated with ways to 'fix' our appearance, very little value is put on the way we think, feel and relate to those around us.

Because there is so much more media to consume and so many more ways in which to consume it we are engaging with images of beauty and perfection, in some cases, more often and more deeply than we engage with the people with whom we work and live. And their very ubiquity means that we begin to see these professionally made-up, Photoshopped and perfectly lit images not only as real, but as normal and attainable, leaving us constantly feeling that we don't measure up. We are conditioned to compare, but it's one thing comparing yourself to a friend or colleague and something very different comparing yourself to what are effectively CGIs (computer-generated images) of celebs that may as well be cartoons, they are that unrealistic. And the upshot of all this comparing is that we become trapped in a situation where we are progressively more and more critical of our appearance, developing a bipolar relationship with our mirror, seeking it out obsessively or trying to avoid it altogether.

Another problematic idea that seems to be evolving in our appearance-orientated culture is the notion that our bodies should be ongoing self-improvement projects – 'works in progress' that we are doomed never to complete. There is always the next new diet, medical procedure or workout that holds the promise of giving us the body and/or life that we so desperately have convinced ourselves that we want. We've bought into the myth that if only we had the right nose or the right breasts, then life would somehow be better. Yet as someone who works in the area of BI and medical psychology I can tell you that over the years I have seen people with facial disfigurements who have better body image and self-esteem than some of the models and actors I have worked with. Because what it all comes down to is how closely your identity and worth as an individual are bound up in appearance. Self-esteem and body image reside in your head, not in your face or body, and any real attempt to feel better about your appearance needs to take into account thoughts and feelings as well as looks.

Part of the problem with the images that envelop our world is the limiting portrayals of women depicted in the media. Most are young and white, slim and attractive.

Hollywood and TV rarely feature women over forty, and those older women who are around tend to look much younger than they are. In *Miss Representation*, Gloria Steinem explained why so many of the women we see on screen are young, while this is not the case for men. She said: 'A male-dominant system values women as childbearers, so it limits their value to the time that they are sexually and reproductively active and they become much less valuable after that.' In other words, as long as we are attractive and biologically viable we are allowed to have a presence on screen, but with the first indication that this is over, or if we don't fit the thin, beautiful ideal in the first place, then the message is clear: no one wants to look at that.

Imagine only seeing thin, attractive men on TV – none of the erudite news reporters, business leaders or politicians, none of the serious actors or musicians – just thin, young, pretty male eye candy. Now think of the impact on our expectations of men – how it would distort their ideas of success and worth. This is what we have been doing to women for decades. And it needs to stop.

Research suggests that thin women are over-represented on TV shows, with only 5 per cent of women on sitcoms being overweight.[10] In fact, according to the researchers, when larger women appear on screen, they tend to draw negative comments from other characters about their looks, and these comments are almost inevitably followed by canned laughter, which cues the viewer to laugh at them as well. And it's not just sitcoms – primetime dramas and reality TV shows have been found to have similar effects through reinforcing the connection between external attractiveness and thinness and positive internal traits.[11] In fact, a 2011 study found that girls who regularly watch reality TV are more likely to consider appearance as the most important thing about themselves.[12]

One of the most shocking studies in this area comes from Canada's Center for Media and Digital Literacy. They note that movies – even those aimed at young children – rarely depict women's bodies realistically. They cite a 2008 study that found that female characters in G-rated animated films (for general viewing) were actually *more* likely to have thin waists and large chests than characters in live-action films or even characters in R-rated movies (for over-eighteens)![13]

Researchers have also found that it's not just the current level of media exposure that influences us, but also its cumulative effects.[14] In fact, as the media's representation of what an 'ideal' body looks like has become progressively thinner over the past fifty years, studies have found statistically significant associations between exposure to these images and body dissatisfaction.[15]

The media is a hugely powerful instrument of change. It affects attitudes, which influence behaviours, which underlay the social norms and beliefs that we live with. Media shapes society and it shapes discourse. And it's everywhere; there is such a diversity of media platforms today that it is practically inescapable. So being aware of the agenda behind those messages is imperative.

The political economy of the media whereby women are sold perfect images so that they can feel bad about themselves and then buy a product to 'fix' themselves is not new.

What is new is how we depict perfection. The digital-enhancement techniques that exist today allow us to lengthen, shorten, lighten and, well, perfect every imperfection. What is really ironic is that editors at major magazines now say that they frequently retouch models who are 'frighteningly thin' to make them look 'less ill'.

In her article on what is actually being edited out of magazine photos sociologist Lisa Wade notes that editors are facing a dilemma between depicting unhealthy images of emaciated models or having to edit photos to amend sunken-in cheeks, protruding collar bones and skinny arms.[16] Friends of mine who are magazine editors talk about airbrushing images of very thin models, and their worry that not only would readers find them unattractive, but also that they are bad role models and that showing them as they are would not be appropriate. But they all note the irony here – namely, that by making very thin models look healthier, they are masking the reality for readers of what it means to be underweight: that a very tiny waist is usually accompanied by a gaunt face, dark circles and protruding bones. By editing these features out, they are feeding the fallacy that being underweight can be healthy and glamorous.

We need more transparency when it comes to pictures; one of the things that I have campaigned for is a symbol showing that a photo has been edited – because whether you are making fat bodies thin or thin bodies fat, you are in effect selling a lie, and coming clean about this would, I believe, have a significant impact on how we internalise the reality of those images.

In the advertising, fashion and beauty industries the same body type is selected over and over again precisely because it is able to sell the impossible ideals that women are supposed to live up to. In the words of the iconic fictional character Bridget Jones:

> ... it's a bit like if we were on a planet where all the space creatures were short, green and fat. Except a very few of them were tall, thin and yellow. And all of the advertising was of the tall, yellow ones, airbrushed to make them even taller and yellower. So all the little green space creatures spent the whole time feeling sad because they weren't tall, thin and yellow.[17]

And that's the thing: we aren't comparing ourselves with our friends and colleagues and neighbours; we aren't even comparing ourselves to real women. Instead, we are comparing ourselves to the idealised notion of what a woman *should* look like, which is very often derived from the not so noble intention to sell us stuff!

The idea that the media and advertisers are just giving us what we want is simply not true; they are giving us what they want to give us – aspirations, insecurities and all.

Create Your Own Brand

There is no doubt that BI impacts on our self-esteem and quality of life. Indeed, there is no question that our appearance always has and will continue to play a part in how others perceive us – it is human nature. But what has changed in the past few years is the fact that the way we look has become central to our self-concept and self-worth, trumping everything else, from our intellect to our passions and beliefs.

One of the things that I find most worrying is the negative self-talk and verbal abuse that women will direct at their bodies, the problem with this being that it escalates: 'I hate my thighs' turns into 'I hate my legs'; then 'I hate my legs' turns into 'I hate my body'; and, eventually, 'I hate my body' inevitably turns into 'I don't like who I am'. In fact, in my work on psychodermatology we have found that negative thoughts can actually have an adverse impact on physical health, causing the deterioration of skin conditions.[18]

I do an exercise with women in my clinics where I get them to look in the mirror and tell me what they like about themselves and it never ceases to amaze me how hard they find it. Yet when I ask them to do the opposite they are able to reel off a raft of things that they don't like, that need 'fixing' or are not right. This is because we are so conditioned to focus on the negative aspects of our appearance that it becomes the only thing we see about ourselves – and only seeing the negative is dangerous. Make a point – a conscious effort – to never leave the mirror without taking note of at least one thing that you like about your appearance. This will start to break down the self-bullying and negative self-talk that so many of us have got used to living with. And while you're at it, start thinking of your body in terms of its functionality, not just in terms of aesthetics. For example, when you eat a piece of cake, don't think about how naughty you are and how it's going to make you fat – enjoy the damned cake! By actually enjoying it as opposed to stressing about it you are more likely to eat less and savour it more.

Our beauty-obsessed culture is conducive to self-objectification; this leads to body shame, which can cause depression, eating disorders and even sexual problems.[19] But you have a choice. You don't have to accept the processed, unrealistic, monolithic images of beauty that surround you as a gauge for personal fulfilment. You can choose to challenge them, rather than measure yourself against them; you can choose to define beauty on your own terms. Women have been doing it for years – from Cindy Crawford refusing to have the mole on her top lip removed to Kim Kardashian embracing her curves; if you decide to love the parts of you that are different and unique, instead of letting them hold you back, those little idiosyncrasies can begin to define you and your own brand of beauty.

One positive and important point to note is that while body dissatisfaction can also affect women who describe themselves as feminists, being a feminist seems to serve a protective purpose in terms of how far we are prepared to go to alter our appearance. For example, women and girls who describe themselves as feminists are less willing to use drastic measures like vomiting to control their weight.[20] Perhaps this has to do with a healthy sense of entitlement – the idea that exploring what it means to be a woman through feminism (or any other paradigm that gets you to think about who you are as an individual, rather than a collection of physical attributes) makes you more resilient to the overriding message that women should seek to satisfy arbitrary societal ideals at any cost. We definitely need all the help we can get to fight the new normalcy of body hate that affects so many women.

The more we strive for the elusive 'perfect', the more we look to see how we measure up – and when, inevitably, we don't measure up, we become more anxious and disparaging, not only about our appearance, but also about our self-worth as human beings. You are beautiful enough to ask of life what you want – don't waste time investing in the one thing that, frankly, will fade faster than everything else that you like (or should like) about yourself.

Disordered Eating

A few months ago I was working in New York. The TV was on in the background in my hotel room as I was getting ready to go out, and I remember it dawning on me that almost every commercial was either about food or weight loss, flogging either the most decadent chocolate chip cookie or some sort of barbell, guaranteed to get rid of your muffin top in record time (and in three easy payments). This mixed up 'Eat/Don't eat' message seems to be everywhere.

Here in the UK too there are whole TV networks devoted to cooking and eating, *X-Factor*-style contests about cupcakes and bakers being turned into pin-ups! This fetishisation of food and concurrent deification of the thin ideal is complicating our relationship with not only how we look but also how we eat.

The number of people diagnosed with an eating disorder in the UK has increased by 15 per cent since 2000, according to a study by King's College London and the UCL Institute of Child Health.[21] This study indicated a 60 per cent increase in females with eating disorders (known as Eating Disorders Not Otherwise Specified or EDNOS) and a 24 per cent increase in males, while figures from the National Institute for Health and Care Excellence suggest that 1.6 million people in the UK are affected by an eating disorder. One point four million of these are female.

Of all those with an eating disorder it is estimated that 10 per cent are anorexic, 40 per cent are bulimic and the rest fall into the EDNOS category. This is really interesting, because while the clinical and diagnostic conditions of a full-blown eating disorder may not be met, that doesn't mean that there isn't an issue; in fact, it is precisely when a condition isn't clinically acknowledged that more complicated eating, denial and a reluctance to seek help may occur.

A person with EDNOS might, for example, meet most of the criteria for anorexia nervosa except for the fact that they are still getting regular periods or that despite significant weight loss their current weight is within the normal range. Or they might meet the criteria for bulimia nervosa, but for the fact that binges occur less frequently than twice a week or have been happening for less than three months. Or perhaps their body weight is normal because they control it through laxative use, over-chewing and spitting out or self-induced vomiting.

According to a survey on body image in *Psychology Today*, 13 per cent of women and 4 per cent of men say they go to extreme measures to restrict their weight by inducing vomiting[22]; people are routinely seeing self-induced vomiting and laxative use as normal and accepted methods of weight control!

If you recognise this kind of behaviour in either yourself of someone you know, it's really important that you (or they) seek professional advice. The sooner a person gets help for eating disorders the better their chances of recovery. Your first port of call should be your GP, who can advise on treatment options, including counselling and therapy. The point is that, left untreated, disordered eating becomes a way of life that can ultimately harm you both physically and mentally, so professional support is essential in order to ensure that it doesn't get to that point.

The weight-ing game

One of the things that complicates our beliefs around weight loss is that we are constantly sold the idea that with the right conviction and willpower we can achieve any body type that we want. However, according to research, this might not actually be the case. Diets are a 50-billion-dollar-a-year industry, yet they don't work; if they did, you would follow one, lose the weight and keep it off for good. Instead, most people end up in a vicious cycle of diet after diet which may produce results in the short term, but not the lasting, clinically significant results needed to make a real difference.

Research in this area suggests that not only lifestyle but genetic and biological factors play a big part as well.[23] When you are on a diet the part of your brain that controls weight – your hypothalamus – doesn't necessarily 'know' that you are trying to lose weight. This is relevant because our hypothalamus has a target for our weight called the 'set point' which is actually determined by our genes, and it aims for this target by constantly assessing how much fat we have in our system and regulating our appetite accordingly.[24]

From a purely biological standpoint, women's bodies need a certain amount of fat to prepare them for the possibility of pregnancy and a healthy baby at some point. But there is an evolutionary reason, too. Back when we were running around in loin cloths trying to catch or gather our food we didn't have three regular meals a day as we do now – we either had lots of food or none at all, so storing fat was essential for survival. When we go on a diet our brains think that we are getting fewer calories because food is scarce, so as soon as we come off the diet and begin to eat normally again it ensures that we eat more than usual, just in case our food sources run out again. This process is actually reinforced the more often we go on a diet and the result is that our brains begin to believe that our food supply is unreliable and so try to protect us by raising the set point.[25] This makes it harder and harder for us to lose weight.

So while our diet and exercise regimes can certainly affect how our bodies look up to a point, they can only work within the parameters that our genes dictate. Our genetic predisposition to how and where we store fat on our bodies cannot be ignored and yet we rarely recognise or talk about this. And herein lies the problem; because, if this isn't acknowledged, the message remains that you aren't trying hard enough to look the way you 'should'. And if you haven't managed to get the body you want, you are left feeling ashamed – and feelings of shame are never conducive to good emotional health.

The notion that weight loss is aspirational has become increasingly dominant over the past few decades. A study that looked at the *Ladies Home Journal* from the 1960s found an average of one diet article every six months,[26] whereas today there are several magazines, TV shows, apps, blogs and websites dedicated entirely to the pursuit of the perfect body. The irony is that confidence in who we are as individuals would make us happier than any diet ever could.

And it's not only size that concerns society when it comes to idealised notions of female appearance. The flawless Photoshopped images in ads and popular media mean that using cosmetics has become not just commonplace, but necessary if we are to feel groomed and presentable. And while I don't object to the use of cosmetics *per se* – it's fun to experiment with fashion or hairstyling, and they can give you a boost – there is a worry in terms of how much of a 'boost' we derive from them, as opposed to other things that could positively influence our confidence.

According to a report in the *Huffington Post*, students in the UK are spending around £1000 a year on beauty products, despite the burden of student loans.[27] And in America women spend more on beauty and fitness than on education.[28] This is indicative of how we have come to believe that looking good means we are somehow better adjusted as individuals; that in this time of disillusionment with the big institutions – from religion to government – beauty has somehow become a moral imperative, and looking good has become synonymous with being good. In a great infographic from the cosmetics website Feel Unique, global comparisons were made on how beauty is related to happiness by looking at what each country spends on it and then comparing that with a 'life satisfaction' survey. America was number one in cosmetics spending, yet ranked twenty-third in the world for satisfaction with life, while Japan, which was number two in cosmetics spending, ranked *ninetieth* in life satisfaction. What's really interesting is that the Netherlands and Sweden, the two countries which spend the least on hair care and makeup, ranked highest when it came to life satisfaction.[29] I should note here that I don't think there is anything wrong with investing in keeping your skin, hair and body looking good, but it's a problem of proportion. We have reached a point where worth and identity are so enmeshed with our physicality that we see physical transformation as the most obvious and efficacious means of self-improvement or even self-empowerment – and that is dangerous. It's dangerous because it distorts our attitudes, affects our behaviour and defocuses us from other perhaps more pertinent issues that may be impacting our sense of wellbeing.

Body Image and Mental Health

Being overly concerned with body image is clearly not the best thing for our mental health, yet the time and energy spent on agonising about appearance, not only as individuals but as a society, suggests this 'concern' is almost obsessive. Some argue that this focus is the result of the consumerist society that we live in, which fosters narcissim; the fact that we are so aware of indicators of beauty and success when it comes to appearance – like the right weight, the right skin tone and the right dress – that these become a way of showing each other that we are 'worthy'. When everything else feels out of control in our lives the numbers on the scale can give us a quantifiable sense of accomplishment.

It's not surprising, therefore, that body dissatisfaction can have a really negative impact on physical and mental health, resulting in depression, low self-esteem, binge-eating and the use of unhealthy weight-control behaviours. One of the things that seems to have a particularly bad effect on our BI is how we speak about ourselves. Researchers have found that the more we engage in self-deprecating 'fat talk' the more likely we are to be dissatisfied with our bodies. Researchers from Trinity University surveyed women between the ages of eighteen and eighty-seven and found that those who reported higher levels of 'fat talk' and 'old talk' tended to have poorer body image. Quite simply, berating yourself for not being thin enough or pretty enough will affect how you behave around others, your decision-making and your confidence.

Another issue that seems to go hand in hand with poor BI is that of perfectionism. The perceived need to be it all and have it all is becoming a genuine concern, and researchers have found that it can actually be predictive of body dissatisfaction and eating disorders.[30] Researchers have identified two aspects of perfectionism that are of most concern: adaptive perfectionism (which relates to the high standards that drive a person towards achieving a goal body image) and maladaptive perfectionism (concerned with avoiding mistakes and with other people's opinions). They found that women who try to achieve a low BMI or low body size were more concerned about making mistakes, had higher self-doubt and were more anxious about general organisational issues than others. We are under relentless pressure to achieve and live up to ridiculously high ideals, and this is worrying, especially as the results of the study suggest a correlation between the two.

Perhaps surprisingly, the mental-health condition with the highest mortality rate is not depression, but eating disorders. In fact, it is estimated that around 20 per cent of sufferers actually die from their condition, so being able to predict who is most likely to develop an eating disorder is imperative if we are going to be able to treat patients. Ultimately, it comes down to recognising that we don't achieve body confidence by getting the 'perfect' body; we achieve it by embracing the body we have.

Selfie, Selfie on the Wall

How others perceive us has always played a role in how we develop our identity.

Back in the day, we generally interacted with people we met in our social and professional circles – in most cases, a limited number of people at any one time who would react not only to our appearance, but also to what we had to say and other social cues. Today, with the advent of the selfie and all the photos we post and share online, huge numbers of people are uniformly and simultaneously reacting to our looks, thus strengthening the impact that others have on how we value ourselves.

Selfies allow us to control how others see us by giving us a choice as to how we present ourselves. And given that research suggests that the profile pictures we post on Facebook can affect not only our perceived physical attractiveness, but also our social and professional attractiveness,[27] it is no surprise that we are all trying desperately to snap that perfect pic. In fact, a recent survey from the American Academy of Facial Plastic and Reconstructive Surgery found that one in three plastic surgeons has seen an increase in people wanting facial procedures so they could look better *online* (a 10 per cent rise in nose jobs, a 7 per cent rise in hair transplants and a 6 per cent rise in eyelid surgery between 2012 and 2013).[31]

The whole psychological and behavioural process of taking, assessing and posting a selfie means that we are becoming much more self-critical, scrutinising and analysing the minutiae of our appearance. Sociologist Ben Agger describes the trend of selfies as 'the male gaze gone viral'. To a large extent, the way that young women pose on social networking sites has a lot to do with what they think they are expected to look like; the pornification of culture has influenced how women see themselves, and given that the overriding message tends to be that a woman's core desire should be to *be desired*, it is no surprise that the duck-face innocent pout, usually paired with grown-up cleavage, is the image of choice. When we post we generally want others to see the best version of ourselves (positive comments like '#gorge' are validating); however, if we feel we *need* that sort of validation from others in order to feel OK about ourselves, it's not healthy.

This need for approval can get out of hand. In the recent trend of 'Am I pretty?' videos which began in the US, young girls posted videos of themselves on YouTube asking strangers to comment on their appearance, with responses ranging from things like 'You're ugly and should die' to 'You're cute, but maybe think of losing weight/fixing your nose' and 'Do your parents know you're doing this?'

In the current climate, the way we feel about our bodies has very little to do with how we actually look and so much more to do with the values that culture and society dictate. However, as normal as it is to compare and seek validation, one of the best things that you can do for your body image is decide that your opinion matters more than anyone else's.

The way that technology affects mental health is fascinating. Working with eating and body-image disorders I find more and more that people come in to see me armed with their Instagram accounts, their favourite pro-ana or pro-mia websites (online communities dedicated to diets and 'thinspiration') and even Facebook comments, by way of explaining and contextualising the way they feel about their bodies. The gadgets we use have become digital prostheses or extensions of who we are: social networking sites provide a virtual environment in which body-image concerns can be categorised and analysed, supported and even challenged, while trends and fads move so quickly online that new terms like #thighgap #boxgap or #bikini-bridge evolve from juvenile catchphrases to genuine measures of physical beauty and worth.

So we're no longer saying simply that looking slim or toned is good; what we are now saying is: 'You know that area between your vagina and the top of your thighs? You need to selectively lose weight there!' And these ridiculous, arbitrary ideals are then normalised and perpetuated through the multitude of images online which, by virtue of their sheer number, can make anything look not only achievable but expected. I'm not certain which is worse: the idea that only one shape and size is beautiful or the newer, more nuanced deconstruction of the female form that fixates on tiny parts of you, but either way, both ensure that you are never fully satisfied with how you look.

Pro-ana and pro-mia images showing girls with skeletal figures, hashtagged #thynspo, #ana or #mia, enable engagement in a virtual community in which insecurities around appearance and weight may be shared. These sites create a sense of belonging by validating experiences through comments on photos, along with supposedly 'helpful' tips on how to achieve similar figures. For example, 'Eating a thin sliver of apple as a replacement for other meals three times a day will help you achieve that gorgeous box gap' or 'Starvation for perfection'. We already know that social comparison is normal, but comparisons on social media are problematic. Because anyone can post anything online, regardless of their experience, knowledge or motivation – the internet is a great democratiser – seeking 'norms' and endorsement of our beliefs (about ourselves and others) online is always going to be risky.

So Now What?

In case you hadn't noticed, pretty doesn't last for ever. So if you put all of your self-esteem eggs into the appearance basket you are going to feel a huge part of your identity and value slipping away as you grow older. Instead, invest time in your education, creativity, passions and beliefs – they will be with you for a lot longer than flawless skin and perky boobs.

If you find you are engaging in negative self-talk, try the strategies on page 44–5. And if you think you are starting to think about food too much, are restricting food intake or getting anxious about what you eat or your weight, then be honest with yourself and seek the help of your GP. The sooner you deal with disordered eating, the better your chances of treating it and getting back in control of your life.

Opting out of the diet game is essential. I had an email from a twenty-three-year old woman a few weeks ago who said that going out with her friends for a meal had become really difficult: 'They all seem to be on diets – one doesn't eat fats, the other doesn't eat carbs, the other doesn't eat after 6pm; all they talk about is how much weight they lost or hope to lose. It's getting ridiculous and frankly I'm worried that it's actually affecting my relationship with food.' My advice is not to buy into the myth that you need to be thin to be happy – we all have a healthy weight we should strive for and this does not translate into a size 6 for all women. Furthermore, fad diets don't work – so instead of dieting, make a conscious decision to eat healthier as a way of life, which simply means less processed stuff, less seeing food as a reward and normal portion sizes. Finally – and perhaps most importantly – be honest with yourself and with your friends: you are all in the same boat and, no doubt, feeling similarly, so instead of competing and complicating nights out, make a pact that when you meet up it should be about your friendships and your relationships, not about food; make your friendships a diet-free zone to help shift the focus on to what really matters.

Also, remember to stay media savvy! Interviewing Style Rookie blogger Tavi Gevinson on the American late-night TV show *The Colbert Report* in January 2013, Stephen Colbert captured the essence of the media's effect on women with the killer question: 'Your magazine actually has positive images for girls, positive messages for girls. But if girls feel good about themselves, how are we gonna sell them things they don't need?'

Learn to separate fantasy from reality, looking at the pictures and promises with a critical eye. You can still admire them, but remember that even the girls in the photos don't look like the girls in the photos!

And speaking of media savvy, if I hear one more advertiser or politician talk about 'real women' I'll scream! Real women can be thin or fat or short or tall or anything in between. Let's stop vilifying each other's body type, wherever we are on the spectrum.

Your body is an amazing instrument that lets you interact with and experience the world around you, so treat it with respect. Eat, move, be healthy and this will have a positive impact on you both physically and mentally. Remember, we all experience negative comments – that's inevitable – but what matters is how we choose to react to them. The fact is that you need to give someone permission before they can make you feel inadequate.

I like to think of body image as being like a pair of glasses. When we are very little the glasses are nice and clean and we can see clearly what is in front of us. But as we grow older the lenses begin to get smudged. Some of the smudges come from bullies telling us we're ugly, some may come inadvertently from our parents, comparing us unfavourably to siblings and friends and some come from the media constantly telling us what we're not. Eventually, we are no longer able to see who we are – only who we are not.

If you want to feel good about your body, you need to start by changing your mind. Change the way you see and value yourself; challenge the rubbish and the lies that will, no doubt, continue to confront you and every woman out there. Don't be beholden to the pursuit of perfection – physical or otherwise; it is self-defeating. Know who you are and be clear that you don't need validation from anyone else to feel good about yourself.

Engage with life and with whatever you are doing from within – you are not directing a photoshoot starring yourself; this is your life, so actively live it, rather than trying to edit it so that it looks OK to others.

You can be more, do more and are worth so much more than just being pretty. You don't have to be pretty if you don't want to be, and equally you should not have to apologise for liking lip gloss or heels, if that's the case. But pretty should never be the *only* thing that defines you.

CHAPTER 3

●

Online Me – Offline Me: Who Am I Supposed to Be?

'I spend hours thinking about what picture I should put up of myself on FB. You don't want to look like you're trying too hard, but then again you want it to look really . . . you know . . . you want to project the kind of lifestyle that you know you should be living – even if you're really not.'

Melissa, aged twenty-two

One of the things I've noticed recently is how there seem to be scripts for everything – not just for how to look or what to wear but, more worryingly, how to act and respond to things. It is as if everything is experienced secondhand, so the 'appropriate' reaction isn't coming from a place of genuine emotional consideration, but rather from a quick, clinical search of 'what the cool girl in a movie' would do.

In a world that is saturated with so much access not

only to information, but also behavioural narratives it is inevitable that, to some extent, our reactions are not personal, but rather dictated by what we think is expected from us. For the first time, arguably, in history, all experience – and our reactions to it – is somehow derivative. It is unusual to live through anything today for the first time without having previously seen it in some other form: before we visit the Louvre, we've seen a hundred depictions of the Mona Lisa; before we see the weary-looking lion at the zoo we've seen endless footage of majestic big cats on the Discovery channel, with cool backtracks and great commentary. And that's the thing – in a way, the secondhand experience is often kind of better. We're used to the edited versions of what is real, complete with the right lighting and background music, so that when they're not there – well, the experience is somehow a bit of a letdown. So we stare at the wonders of the world just a little underwhelmed.

But what I think is more worrying is not the big stuff, the impersonal stuff – it's the things we are supposed to experience firsthand but don't. We see a thousand first kisses before we experience our own. We have catchphrases for what to say when we're in love, like 'You complete me'; and when we want to break up – 'It's not you, it's me'. We know the appropriate facial expressions to make when having sex and when making love (the proliferation of porn online has ensured that any nuanced differences are no longer nuanced). We know not only how to act, but even how to move between roles – Diazesque 'cool girl', Megan Foxish 'hot girl'. And we don't take things at face value, but rather have detailed scripts for everything we experience – the 'shoulds' and 'have-tos' that surround popular culture today are substantially more detailed and come with intricate flow charts detailing our movements, behaviours and attitudes. But perhaps most worryingly they make us relate to ourselves as outsiders, looking in on our own experience. And the question then is this: if we are scanning our pop-culture-drenched psyches for what we should say and who we should be, then are we ever really aware of what it is we actually want?

Identity

Who am I? It's a question as old as, well, consciousness, I guess. The need to come to an understanding of what makes us unique, how others identify us and how we see ourselves is central to our emotional health. It encompasses the totality of the knowledge that we hold about our personalities, capabilities, interests and relationships. More than that, identity is not just about who we think we are today, but who we think we can be in the future, and it is these self-conceptions that act as the aspirations and goals towards which we ultimately strive. The way we think of ourselves defines who we become, and the directions our lives take.

When we have a healthy sense of who we are, we are more likely to push ourselves, venture out of our comfort zones and explore the limits of our abilities. It gives us a healthy sense of entitlement and affiliation, so that while we can feel good about our uniqueness we can also feel we are an integral part of a group.

An interesting point about identity construction is how we go about developing it. We look at two things: we look at ourselves and we look at the world around us and, through these, we try and figure out who we are supposed to be. Now because people are fundamentally social beings, making sense of where we fit in socially and culturally is vital. Identity therefore needs to be internally and externally congruent, meaning that the view we have of ourselves is consistent with feedback we get about ourselves from others.

But with technological advances and social changes, our social worlds have expanded dramatically, making the whole area of identity construction more complicated. In the last few years our core influences have changed from being limited, more or less, to people we come into direct contact with to almost limitless access to and interactions with people online. So it's not surprising that a wider range of factors are influencing the development of our self-concept than ever before.

This has caused a shift in identity construction, from its being internally driven ('This is who I am') to externally driven ('This is who I am supposed to be'). And whereas previously this process was a rite of passage in adolescence, the need to constantly define it and be defined by it, means that it is affecting us well into our twenties and beyond.

The Social-media Mirror

Popular culture manufactures 'portraits' of who it wants us to be, drawing on our basic need for social acceptance and often bearing no relation to who we really are. After all, an identity that is shaped by popular culture is there to serve its own best interests, not ours.

And this is where the whole social networking thing gets interesting. Social media has become as much about defining our identity as it is about connecting with friends and family. The need to establish a presence, an identity that people take note of, may explain why we feel it's necessary to incessantly share every *positive* detail about our lives. 'Look at me on the beach with a crazy big cocktail in Spain!' 'Here's my new selfie – pouting 'cause I'm bored (and because I look good pouting).' 'Just bought fab new Jimmy Choos! #shoesareagilsbestfriend.' Even the most avid social-media user must find exhausting the incessant need to quantify their identity with cool pics and clever hashtags. The fact is, research shows that that is what social networking sites like Facebook have turned into – places we go to try and measure up.[1]

The way that the majority of social networking sites are set up (and I am referring here to the clap-o-meter element they all share – 'likes', 'followers', etc.) has caused a shift away from expressing who we are and a move towards constructing our personas based on the answer to the question: 'How can I look good to others?' We actively seek out acceptance, popularity, status and, by extension, self-esteem,[2] so that the need to know oneself makes way for the more pressing need to ensure that we manage what others think about us – basically, that we self-promote. And there is an increasing body of research that suggests this is making us feel, well, not so 'liked'.

A new study conducted jointly by the University of Michigan and Leuven University in Belgium has shown that the more someone uses Facebook, the less satisfied they are with life.[3] What's particularly interesting about this research is that, unlike previous investigations which were cross-sectional (in other words, snapshots in time), this study is longitudinal, meaning the researchers have looked at the effects of using Facebook over a longer period. Analysis of the results found that the more a volunteer used Facebook, the worse they reported feeling in terms of mood and over-all life satisfaction as compared to those who visited the site infrequently. In contrast, there was a positive association between the amount of direct social contact a volunteer had and how positive they felt. In other words, the more vol-unteers socialised in the real world, the more positive they reported feeling, whereas the opposite was true for the online world.

For many people Facebook was originally a way of recon-necting with old friends; it was an incredibly effective tool that allowed us to contact people who, due to geography or even apathy, we'd lost track of. It was community-building, and it felt good to keep a lot of these people in our lives. But research shows that now it is much less about community-building or reconnecting and more about comparing. In fact, social psychologists suggest that when we aren't sure about how well we're performing, we look to the people around us to help us decide if what we are doing measures up – something called Social Comparison Theory, originally proposed in 1954 by Leon Festinger (more about this later – see page 69). And therein lies the appeal of social networking:

it provides an easy way to 'grade' yourself in comparison to others, which is where the social surveillance begins, with people spending more time looking at others' pages than adding to their own.

But here's the thing – the more information we have about what people think of us, the more likely it is that our identities will be not expressions of our genuine selves, beliefs and values, but the products of traits that either we would like to have or that we assume others want to see in us. So identity no longer gives us a sense of individuality, containment and belonging; instead, it serves as a means to seek acceptance from other people, some of whom we don't even really know. And if we are always tweaking who we are as a means of satisfying our 'friends' and 'followers', it stands to reason that deep down we don't believe we are actually worthy of being liked or of being accepted for who we really are.

To complicate things further, we now have access to information about what everyone thinks about us. So the amorphous 'They' – 'What will *They* think?' or '*They* say that it's good to . . .' – well, they're not so amorphous any more. *They* are actually out there. *They* 'like' us on Facebook or 'follow' us on Twitter. *They* comment on our photos and on our thoughts. *They* are the masses who are now able to communicate with us and tell us what they think of who we are. *They* have begun to matter like never before.

The importance that we place on the perceptions of people we don't even know is particularly telling in the results of research showing that, when forming perceptions of others online, we tend to rely more on 'other-generated' than 'self-generated' information. In other words, opinions of other people matter more than our own self-presentation. So for social networking users who want to make a certain impression, being aware of how others are responding to and commenting about them is paramount in achieving a positive self-presentation – this, of course, perpetuates the idea that we need to conform to the expectations of others in order to be accepted.[4]

To complicate things further, if *They* are now more tangible and have a louder voice, then their effect on the manner in which we socially construct our identities becomes particularly relevant. Add to this the fact that every online company from Amazon to Netflix is telling us what we should like, what products and services a person 'like you' will enjoy, and all of a sudden it's not the people around you, your family and friends – the people who know you best and have your best interests at heart – who are defining your identity; instead, it's those who don't know you, but just want to sell you stuff! So the concept of *They* is then even more significant, as it's not just about how we are perceived, but about how we ought to react to the world around us – what we should like, enjoy, engage in.

Will the Real Me Please Stand Up

Because we are so aware that social networking is about building our special kind of brand, we are all very 'on message' with regard to what that 'brand' should be. A large-scale study that looked into this, found that over 75 per cent of the people they asked said they shared only 'good things' with their communities on social-networking sites. So while wanting to live up to societal expectations – promoting ourselves, our lifestyles in a way that complies with what society deems worthy or acceptable – is nothing new, what is different is the fact that we feel our lives are more visible because they are online. Our online profiles mean that we are engaging with people even when we are not there. And whereas a simple 'Yep, nothing new' would work fine in the context of a face-to-face interaction, in our online lives we feel the need to update constantly with ever more detail. And this, combined with the visual superficiality of the online world, means that we look to archetypal indicators of success as a means of conveying how well we're doing.

A study from Humboldt University in Germany found that the most common emotion aroused by using Facebook is envy.[5] Endless comparisons with doctored photographs and amplified achievements can, unsurprisingly, leave us feeling low about ourselves and envious of others. In many ways the need to impress our peers never really leaves us and exposure to old high-school friends on Facebook doesn't help.

We are all almost programmed to compare – we are socialised into it. So the mark we get in a test, for example, doesn't really mean anything in itself; it's how we rank in relation to the rest of the class that matters to us. According to Social Comparison Theory, we are all driven to gain accurate evaluations of ourselves by comparing ourselves to others in order to reduce uncertainty about how we are perceived and through this we define who we are. The reason we seek out these comparisons is because they provide an objective benchmark against which we can judge ourselves in different areas, giving us a sense of validity and cognitive clarity.[6]

Now there are two ways we compare ourselves. *Downward* social comparison is a defensive tendency that we use for self-evaluation. We look to another person or group whom we consider to be worse off in order to dissociate them from ourselves and because it makes us feel better about who we are. It probably explains why all those 'Look-at-her-cellulite-isn't-it-awful' magazine features are so popular. Then there is *upward* social comparison. Research suggests that comparisons with others who are better off or superior can lower self-esteem. And it is these upward comparisons that we tend to seek out online – especially when we're feeling low.[7] We compare upwards because we want to see ourselves as special – as somehow better or superior – so we evaluate ourselves in terms of these ideal groups that we think we *should* be like. And so online we are all portraying our 'ideal' selves: the best photos, the best dinners, the trips … it's the superlatives of each other's lives that we are using as benchmarks. And we make upward comparisons both consciously and subconsciously, so often we aren't even aware that we are making them.

Decades of research on body image tells us that comparing our bodies to the airbrushed photographs of models in magazines makes us feel bad about ourselves,[8] and the same is true of upward comparisons on social networking sites. To complicate things even further, research has also shown that we tend to spend more time online when we're feeling low or lonely, which means we are more likely to see the fabulous, well-edited lives of friends and family at a time when we are feeling the lowest about our own. This has given rise to something that researchers call 'FOMO' or 'Fear Of Missing Out'. FOMO is the upshot of seeing friends and family relaxing on holiday or looking amazing at parties while you are at home eating yesterday's leftovers in front of the TV with pimple cream on your face. It's the fear that everyone else is having more fun, more excitement and more anecdote-worthy experiences than you are. And given that your friends' lives, accomplishments and fab experiences are plastered across a multitude of devices, it's easy to feel you're missing out.

The Commercialisation of Identity

The way that identity has been commercialised through movies and TV, and now through social networking, means we're all sort of working to a script, a collective idea of *what needs to happen next*. And it makes the difference between us being real people and an amalgam of personality traits derived from a diet of overused characters; the difference between knowing who we are and who we are *expected* to be. This is particularly relevant to us as women since media representations of womanhood tend to be more constrictive than those for men.

In 2009, Maddy Coy, a lecturer at London Metropolitan

University, asked a thousand girls aged fifteen to nineteen to choose their ideal job from a list of different careers, including things like medicine and teaching. Sixty-three per cent of those asked considered glamour modelling their ideal profession, while a quarter cited lap dancing as their top choice. When I first read this statistic I was surprised; after all, if you could do anything, be anything, would having your picture taken without a top on really be at the top of your list? But of course, decisions and choices don't occur in a vacuum. We make decisions and create belief systems based on the messages around us. And in the hypersexualised landcape of the last decade or so, in which the consistent message has been that a woman's value lies in her youth, beauty and sexual attractiveness, it makes sense to try and amplify those aspects of our identity. Ironically, we tolerate the notion that women should be sexualised and objectified if they want to be because some-how this rests on the illusion of gender equality: if we are all equal, then it is a woman's prerogative to decide to be objectified and to prioritise her sexual availability above anything else, right? Now there is nothing inherently wrong with investing in your attractiveness, sexuality and appearance, if that's what you really want. The problem is that in the current context, where a woman's value is con-sistently bound up with her sexual attractiveness, it's clear that some choices are valued more than others. And this, no doubt, has an effect on what women are choosing and on the beliefs and behaviour of both sexes.

Looking through research on gender studies, one thing that comes up repeatedly is that women are more likely to take risks when they are surrounded by other women. Even as girls, this seems to be the case. In a review of literature from the National Education Association (NEA) in the US, researchers found that girls who learn in all-girl environments tend to be more comfortable responding to questions and sharing their opinions in class and that they are more likely to explore more 'traditionally male' subjects such as maths, science and technology. And, like adult women, they are also more likely to take risks, such as speaking in front of the class, and tend to exhibit higher levels of self-confidence and self-esteem.[9]

The results of a study published in 2012 show that risk-taking in women comes down to 'social learning' and environmental factors, rather than inherent gender traits.[10] The authors of the study designed a controlled experiment using students from years ten or eleven who made choices about real-stakes lotteries in different environments. Students were randomly assigned to either all-female, all-male or mixed gender groups. They found, on average, that women were less likely to make risky choices than men when they were in mixed gender groups, but when assigned to all-female groups women were just as likely to take risks as men. The risk-taking behaviour of men was unaffected by group composition. The researchers of the study note that these findings have significant implications for the labour market. If, on average, women are more risk-averse than men, and if much of the remuneration in high-paying jobs consists of bonuses linked to a company's performance, relatively fewer women will choose high-paying jobs because of the uncertainty.

What this and similar studies show is that risk-taking behaviour is not necessarily innate, but rather can be influenced by a person's environment. In fact, they suggest that even those women who are intrinsically more willing to take risks may avoid doing so because of culturally driven norms and beliefs about how women 'should' behave, although once they are placed in an all-female environment, this inhibition is reduced.

The invisible woman

The effects of underrepresentation of women are everywhere. Female professors are almost 50 per cent less likely than their male counterparts to be invited to join corporate scientific advisory boards (SABs) and start new companies mainly because of gender stereotyping, according to University of Maryland researchers.[11] And according to the authors of the study, assumptions that women lack leadership qualities, are less business savvy and are not capable of helping new ventures attract investment block their advancement in these areas. And it's not that women scientists aren't available – the numbers are there, they are just not being selected. Women have to prove themselves more than men do when it comes to advancement – in fact, a 2011 McKinsey report noted that men are promoted based on potential, whereas women's promotions tend to be based on accomplishments.[12]

And, of course, there are all those depressing stats given by Sheryl Sandberg, COO of Facebook, in a recent Ted Talk and in her book on the inequality of women in the workplace – *Lean In*.[13] She cites that only 20 per cent of non-profit organisations are run by women; in 195 independent countries there are only 17 female heads of state; women hold 20 per cent of seats in government globally; 4 per cent of the Fortune 500 companies are run by women; and – the most striking stat when it comes to our fear of taking risks – 57 per cent of men negotiate salaries, compared with just 7 per cent of women.

One reason that is often given for these figures is the lack of role models. A study published in the May 2013 issue of the *Journal of Experimental Social Psychology* provides a compelling example of how important female role models are to women's performance.[14] One hundred and forty-nine students, comprising eighty-one women and sixty-eight men were each asked to give a speech arguing against higher tuition fees. Some of the students spoke with a poster of Hillary Clinton on the back wall, some with one of Angela Merkel, some with one of Bill Clinton and the rest with no poster at all.

The female students who had images of either Hillary Clinton or Angela Merkel on the wall spoke for significantly longer than those who didn't. Indeed, their speeches were more positively received by observers and rated as higher in quality both by their audience (who weren't aware of the presence of the posters) and the women themselves. The performance of the male students on the other hand was the same, regardless of who was on the poster or whether the posters were in the room or not.

So the correlation between female role models and

women's performance is clear. The trouble is that there are not enough senior female role models in business, and opportunities to meet and be inspired by them directly are few and far between.

To complicate this further we hear about relatively few women who are celebrated for their business acumen or accomplishments in science and industry. In fact, society tends to make celebrities out of mainly one type of woman – the 'sexually desirable' – whose accomplishments (be it performing, singing, being on TV) are seen as a product of this and not of hard work, intelligence or talent. So while we idolise women who fall into this category, we ignore or minimise the achievements and successes of women in the vast majority of other professions.

Where are the editorials about amazing female scientists and explorers? Where are the accolades for female sporting teams? Why aren't we celebrating the young female activists who are out there trying to change the world? We need to transform the way we celebrate women and we need to do it soon or we risk condensing the value of a generation of women down to the most superficial, meaningless aspects of who they are.

This type of objectification and such hypersexualised female ideals can explain the weak self-esteem, poor self-image and lack of confidence that are so common today, the results of which are clear in the increasingly low aspirations seen in the study cited earlier (see page 72).

Very simply, we get our behavioural scripts from the messages with which we are bombarded most consistently. And the younger and less experienced we are, the harder it is to challenge these scripts, which are currently saying, 'Your value lies in being desired – if you want to succeed, bank on your looks and not your brain. Be a WAG not a Ph.D.'

Take the 2013 series of *The Apprentice* as an example. The female candidates – who just happened to be attractive – were just as competent as the male contestants, yet they were judged twice: once on their business talent and then again on their looks. In the press, journalists dubbed them 'glamour girls', saying: 'Sunday's battle of the lovely hair, long legs and manicured nails/talons between Luisa Zissman and Leah "Doc" Totton should prove good value.' As women we are told that because our worth lies in our bodies instead of our brains, we won't make it unless we are desirable and sexy. The media ignores key qualities such as drive, ambition and intelligence — all that matters is that men fancy us.

We are now beginning to see the effects of that message not only for young women, but for men as well. A survey by Onepoll in 2009 found that over 50 per cent of men said brains did not factor in their decision when choosing a mate, as long as she was good-looking because it was important to impress their friends, while eight out of ten said they would be intimidated by a clever woman. And a study from the University of Chicago that looked at online dating preferences found that men displayed a significant bias against women who were more educated than them.[15] So the message here is clear: a woman isn't an equal to challenge men; instead, she is a prize whose appearance reflects on men's value as much as it does on her own.

So Now What?

Now that we have some idea of what we are facing, the question is: what do we do about it? Being clear about who we are – having a strong sense of our own identity – is critical, not only in terms of confidence and self-esteem, but actually with regard to good mental health (see Chapter 2).

The truth is that we all need some sense of direction when deciding who we ought to be. Modern culture leaves us free to decide what to be and what to make of ourselves. But a lot of people argue that the big institutions we used to rely on for a sense of who we are – be it in terms of religion, politics or nationality – are no longer as relevant as they once were, which is why, perhaps, the online world has become so instrumental in guiding us in the construction of identity.

The more choices we have, the less secure we become in those we have already made, and so constructing our identities gets harder and harder. To counter this we need to think about where we are getting our guidance from.

Our world has always 'socially constructed' us to some extent; our families and the cultures we identify with – both nationally and socially – have long played a role in defining who we are. But what we are seeing now is what happens when strangers and impersonal companies with a vested interest in making a profit from us begin to define us. We are seeing what happens when social comparisons are made not with each other in 'real time' or even in 'real life', but with ideal edited online versions of each other. In many cases, we're not even aspiring to emulate real people on- or offline – the people with whom we actually have an affinity, either through direct knowledge or research – but rather the cool fictional characters we see on screen. Ironically, these characters tend to be dreamed up by someone whose mandate is, consciously or not, to create someone who is so 'almost perfect' (because even her imperfections aren't real imperfections – just cool little idiosyncrasies) that guys want to marry her and girls want to be her. But the truth is that most women aren't like the girl in the romcoms: they can't challenge you to competitive-eating competitions while retaining a size-zero body – that is not real life! So when you watch one of these flicks, view it not as you would a documentary on the Discovery channel, but rather as a sci-fi film, remembering that it was probably written by someone who doesn't get out much but has a great imagination!

We need to start thinking about the source when it comes to internalising the guidelines that help us to construct ourselves. It's time to stop listening to *Them* because *They* don't know us. *They* never have. So whether it's the off-the-cuff comment that begins with '*They* say that …' or the more insidious, well-defined *They* who comment on who we are via any number of media, we need to step back and decide how – and how much – we let them affect us.

Think about it like this: to a large degree, online comments pages are like the defaced cubicles in a dodgy restroom that invite anyone with a chewed-up pen to 'have at it'. Social scientists even have a name for this; it's called the 'Online Disinhibition Effect' and involves the loosening or, in some cases, the complete abandonment of the social inhibitions we are used to in normal face-to-face interaction.

So these comments aren't really about you; they say much more about the person at the 'other end' of the keyboard. The notion of letting someone who doesn't even know you take up that much space in your mind or, worse yet, have a say in how you feel about and depict yourself is simply wrong. If you need to test out how you look in the eyes of others, make sure to use someone who actually attempts to really see you, rather than those who project on to you.

Seek out your role models rather than just being handed them. And this is really important because it's easy to be lazy when it comes to this one – to just sit back and look at what (and who) is being celebrated and decide that that's just the way things are. It doesn't have to be that way. There are some amazing women out there doing amazing things, but you need to look for them because – for now, at least – the media seems to want to celebrate women for their physical desirability rather than their accomplishments. So we know way more than we probably want to know about what random reality-TV stars like to eat for breakfast or where they shop, rather than hearing about the businesswomen, the scientists and the political activists who are changing the world.

And remember – wisdom and the sharing of ideas and inspiration are ageless. A woman doesn't have to be at the top of her career to make an effective role model. So look close to home, too; look for what you admire in someone, either a skill or behaviour, and make it your goal to find out how that person acquired that skill and what it would take for you to develop, refine and apply it. All around us are people with traits that we can admire and respect. Seek them out – connect with them.

Finally, remember to read Facebook pages in the way that you'd read press releases. They are edited versions of people's lives and the editors are all trying to figure out what their audience wants and give it to them. I have to say, I think it's so ironic that the way that Facebook started was as a site to compare who had the prettiest face; in some ways it seems to have come full circle.

And don't get me wrong – I don't think that social networking is all bad – what I do think is that it's time we realised that our online identities can impact on who we think we need to be offline as well. In fact, the two worlds are becoming ever more intertwined. As such, it is so important to learn to disconnect from 'false' identities in order to gain the freedom to be who we really are. We need to recognise the identities we're holding on to and then reframe them by speaking about them in a way that creates a sense of 'distance', so lessening our emotional attachment to them.

From existential philosophers to behavioural scientists, the recognition that we all have a desire for authenticity has been around for ever. It is core to our sense of wellbeing, a cornerstone of mental health. Being authentic and true to who we are is correlated with self-esteem, vitality and self-determination. So rewrite your script, on your own terms, looking inwards for what feels right and ignoring those would-be editors who don't know you at all.

•

CHAPTER 4

The Need to Please – Pressure, Expectations and Saying No

'I hate saying no. It's not that I don't want to – it's more that I feel bad if I do because I don't want to let people down. I hate the idea of people thinking badly of me and I hate confrontation too, so I always end up saying yes to stuff and then spend ages regretting it.'

Lizzie, aged twenty-seven

The ancient Greek philosopher Aristotle once said, 'There is only one way to avoid criticism: do nothing, say nothing and be nothing' – yet the need to be liked, accepted by our peers and not to 'rock the boat' is as old as time.

Now, let me be clear that wanting to please people some of the time is OK. Yes, even the type we do through self-interest. Your conscience may tell you that you only helped that old lady across the road to make yourself feel good – but so what? You still did something worthwhile for a fellow human being, and I'm willing to bet that old lady would be very grateful to you for being so 'selfish'.

But people-pleasing becomes an issue when you find yourself so intent on seeking approval from others that you ignore your own needs in an attempt to gain it. In some ways, people-pleasers are actually unable to assess the value of their own decisions and actions and, as such, they are disproportionately interested in whether those around them agree with their decisions, ultimately allowing others to validate their choices.

Wanting the approval of other people is fine, as long as it's balanced with good self-care. In fact, we are hardwired to be nice – because around two million years ago being unpleasant would have left us without the protection of our own species, and possibly in danger of being eaten by another one! But while this group conformity has carried forward to modern society – even today, you don't hear anyone praising the attributes of selfish people (except maybe on reality TV, where narcissists and egotists are essentially celebrated, but that's another story!) – this basic survival instinct has been replaced, in many of us, by a need to please on a superficial level, perhaps as a means to avoid confrontation or to seek approval, regardless of whether this is at odds with our happiness and self-esteem; in other words, the things we really need to survive.

Social psychologists have been fascinated with the concept of group conformity for years. Figuring out how and why we choose to modify our beliefs and behaviours in order to feel part of a group is relevant to everything from bullying to which fashion trends make it big. As far back as

1955, the psychologist Richard Crutchfield defined conformity as 'yielding to group pressures', explaining that such
behaviour is often driven by the simple desire to be liked by
other people. Our perception of what makes us likeable
stems from our childhood: if we are taught that to be liked
is to conform to certain parameters without question, we
will struggle as we grow up – because although our needs
change through life, the subconscious pressure to conform
'whatever it takes' does not.

Back in the 1950s, American psychologist Carl Rogers
argued that a child has two basic needs: self-worth and the
desire for positive regard (to feel respected and loved by
others).[1] Rogers believed that if you have high self-worth, i.e.
you feel confident and positive about yourself, you will be
able to accept failures and times of unhappiness, embrace
challenges and be open with others. On the other hand, if
you have low self-worth, you might shy away from challenges, be unable to accept that sometimes life can be
unhappy and become defensive and guarded towards other
people.

Rogers went on to define two types of positive regard:
unconditional positive regard (where others accept and love
you for what you are, regardless of your actions) and *conditional* positive regard (where the acceptance and love that,
say, a child receives is dependent upon their behaviour).
Someone who has grown up with unconditional positive
regard may feel more able to try new things as an adult, even
if it means getting it wrong sometimes. A child who has
only known conditional positive regard, on the other hand,
will grow up to believe that they will only be loved if they

please other people, and will therefore constantly seek approval and try to meet the needs of others.

As women, we are more likely to become people-pleasers.[2] This is, perhaps, because girls, as children, are typically conditioned to accommodate the views of others.[3] Research has also found that women in general are less likely to take risks (see page 73) and are therefore more likely to go along with the majority because, from an evolutionary perspective, they develop an 'anti-risk' reaction in order to protect their babies. Men, however, have evolved quite differently and actually take risks as a means of establishing their status.[4]

What is interesting is that the belief that we will only be loved if we please others is not just a self-belief, but one that is also held by others, leading them to expect such behaviour from us. And because this people-pleasing behaviour is likely to be rewarded as we grow up, by parents, friends and colleagues, it's really hard to let go of. In fact, the belief eventually becomes self-reinforcing, making people-pleasers ever more eager to care for others to the detriment of themselves in order to win the social reinforcement that they crave.[5]

People-pleasers will go to great lengths to make those around them feel more comfortable, and this eagerness to please can affect many areas of a person's life, as was found by a study in 2012.[6] Researchers looked at the eating habits of college students (forty-one men and sixty women) and found that people-pleasers will overeat in social situations if they think it will make other people feel comfortable. According to the lead author of the study, this compulsion to behave in a way that makes others feel more at ease can be observed in a variety of situations. For example, a people-pleaser may feel stressed or guilty if they consider themselves to be more successful than those around them, in areas as diverse as academia, athletics and even relationships.

Approval Addiction

As children, we need the love and affection of authoritative figures, such as our parents, because this provides us with our security. But while a good parent should instil in their child a sense of their own worth, the balance of responsibility lies with the child. When we eventually move away from home, perhaps to go off to university, we need to take on this responsibility, so that we can be in control of how we are treated by others and their attitudes towards us.[7] The problem is that some of us don't assume this responsibility and instead continue to focus on pleasing everyone as we go through life.

Now, if you adopt this approach it can be satisfying for a while. You may feel that you have a great group of friends, be confident that your boss likes you and your family thinks you're lovely. However, while everyone else seems happy with you, you slowly become aware that one person isn't: you. This feeds your insecurity and gradually you go from thinking, 'I will be liked if I please people' to, 'I *won't* be liked if I *don't* please people'. When you feel insecure, seeking approval is a way of feeling better about yourself, but sometimes this behaviour becomes so habitual that, even when you begin to feel more positive about yourself, you still feel you can't 'let people down' – even if it means that you are ultimately putting unreasonable pressure on yourself.

Interestingly, people-pleasing is not confined to those around us who actually *can* provide us with security, or improve our lives in some way. Very often, we will show compassion to those who need our help – or rather, those whom we *think* need our help – receiving nothing in return but their approval, and that of an imagined audience of our friends and peers. This sounds innocent enough. Noble, even. Yet, we can attach so much importance to approval that we find ourselves wanting it when we don't get it or, worse, when we perceive we have failed. And the irony is that we simply can't show ourselves the same compassion that we show others.

By this point we have become addicted to approval, to the exclusion of balanced thinking. Like a drug, the more we have of it, the more we crave it and the less powerful its effect, until the need for it eclipses all else. And that's when our quality of life begins to suffer. Quite simply, our people-pleasing behaviour starts to have the opposite effect to that which we desire – it pushes people away. To cope with this, we may display a plethora of seemingly harmless (at first) traits and strategies – the kind of behaviour you might expect from a defiant child: sulking, refusing to communicate, being obstructive and so on. Indeed, these forms of passive aggression may well have started in childhood, but manifest themselves in adulthood as the 'Why-don't-you-like-me?' disease.

So, as we can see, very quickly the cycle of people-pleasing leads us to enter into a highly destructive spiral. But, thankfully, breaking this cycle can be relatively straightforward because the chances are we are simply taking things too personally. Very often, we are making negative assumptions about the thoughts, intentions or motives of another person, which are, in fact, nothing more than projections of our own thoughts and feelings, and we see the perceived negative event as a reflection or confirmation of our own personal worthlessness.

The first step towards trying to stop taking things too personally – and we all do it (I know I do!) – is to ask yourself this simple question: 'What does this situation really say about *me*?' Say it out loud if you have to, and it may help you to see that you are actually making negative assumptions about things. If you struggle to depersonalise the situation, ask yourself this: 'What would this say about *my best friend* if she were in this situation?'

Alternatively, keep a 'thought record', noting down your feelings about any situation that you would have liked to have handled differently, and work through how you felt at the time, step by step – from the initial thought, to the negative thinking behind it, to what you think could be the source of that negativity – and then try to challenge those negative beliefs. With practice, you will eventually be able to do this in your head until it becomes subconscious and, dare I say it, rational. The simple act of reducing your 'to-please' list by even just one responsibility will also free up some valuable time for you. And perhaps the most important thing to remember is that genuine approval should be based upon who you are, rather than the favours that you do.

Guilty – as Charged?

Guilt is an interesting emotion that is integral to our need to please. As we have seen, people-pleasing often begins in childhood, and the roots of guilt also take hold when we are young.

Children have an inherent need to be loved by their parents and are conditioned to work hard to get approval from them; if their parents are happy with them, the world feels like a happier, safer place, where they can be relaxed and centred. But the thing is that over time we become conditioned to seek approval not just from our parents, but from everyone around us, as a way of replicating those feelings of safety, calm and acceptance.

When a child does something wrong they are confronted with the disappointment of the adults around them (parents, teachers and so on). In order to win back their approval and stop feeling guilty about disappointing them, they may change their behaviour. But if the parents – consciously or otherwise – elicit guilt as a means of discipline, focusing more on validating good and punishing bad behaviour than on encouraging their child to assert him- or herself, there is a risk that their child will think they are 'bad'.

Being told that we are 'bad' is very different to being told that we have 'done a bad thing'. The former makes us feel a sense of shame and guilt and, unsurprisingly, not only leads to a strong desire to please others – at our own expense – but also to low self-esteem, which only perpetuates the guilt we are feeling and the resulting approval-seeking behaviour. If this method of parenting goes on for long enough, by the time we reach adulthood we have become conditioned to put the needs of others ahead of our own.

The fact that gender-based play patterns tend to make more allowances for 'naughty' behaviour from boys – meaning that 'naughtiness' in boys is somehow expected and therefore more acceptable – may go some way to explaining why guilt tends to be felt more intently by women, as identified by a 2010 study conducted by the University of the Basque Country.[8] This, together with the facts that women are traditionally socialised into caring roles, and that guilt is often associated with caring about our actions, means, as the saying goes, we're damned if we do and damned if we don't!

We are generally taught that if we feel guilty or bad, it means that we care about what we've done. By contrast, if we don't feel guilty or we feel indifferent about something, it means that we don't care. And, of course, not caring makes us 'bad' people.

But here is the thing: *not* feeling guilty doesn't necessarily mean that you don't care. It may simply mean that you are choosing to live by what feels right for *you*, rather than choosing to adhere to social or moral codes that are externally driven and often conflict with your internal codes of right and wrong.

As women, we have an additional layer of external codes to contend with – thanks, ironically, to feminism. As we saw in Chapter 1, the first wave of feminism in the late nineteenth century enabled women to say, 'We *can* have it all', but over time this somehow became, 'We *should* have it all'. This meant that we began to feel guilty if we didn't manage to successfully juggle holding down a career and a healthy, happy relationship – all with perfectly highlighted hair, plucked eyebrows and a body to make Elle Macpherson jealous, obviously!

Guilt, and the discomfort associated with it, leads to the desire to regain approval, and approval from a group is, of course, more likely if we share similar tastes or opinions (which is why things that are popular are so . . . well, popular). But what happens is that, as a means of avoiding the sense of guilt and the negative, uncomfortable feelings associated with it, we repress our own needs and instead focus on those of others, in an attempt to conform to an ideal that will satisfy our parents, partners, friends or society as a whole. As a consequence, we are left living by externally imposed standards that prevent us from expressing our true selves, making us feel unhappy. We lack self-care and become anxious that our true self – the self we are repressing – may be found out.

If we spend our lives trying to please others, we never get a chance to actually engage with what it is that we really want, and to enjoy life. And worse, if our ability to accept ourselves becomes too bound up in what other people think of us, our need to please becomes even greater and our self-esteem becomes dependent on the approval of others. And so, if we don't receive the approval we seek, we feel depressed and anxious.

So what is the point of guilt? Well, it acts as a kind of barometer, telling us if something about our behaviour needs changing, alerting us to the fact that we are doing something that doesn't sit well with our conscience. The question is: do we respond to our conscience? And, if we do, how? How do feelings of guilt affect our behaviour?

According to a 2012 study, when a person feels guilty about something they have done, they either try to make it up to the person they have hurt or try to alleviate their guilt by doing something helpful for someone else.[9] The study also found that because guilt is a very different emotion to 'feeling bad', it can, in moderation and when directed appropriately, actually serve a positive purpose: if you hurt another person, you put your relationship with that person at risk; if you feel guilty about your actions, you tend to show that person generosity, demonstrating that you value your relationship with them.

But how do we put a stop to the guilt we use as a 'go-to' emotion, every time we feel conflicted or engage with a challenging situation?

Saying No

It's such a little word, so why is it sometimes so hard to say? Many of us fear saying no because we think that others will see us negatively – they might think we're lazy, uncaring or selfish. But the thing is, if we are confident and secure enough to know who we are, then it shouldn't matter what other people think.

The author of *Nice Girls Can Finish First*, Daylle Deanna Schwartz, demonstrated how the need to feel like a 'nice person' underlies people-pleasing habits when she appeared on *The Oprah Winfrey Show*. When asked whether they would prefer to be liked or respected, practically every member of the show's audience said they'd rather be liked. And for most of these people, being liked meant pleasing people.

At some level, people-pleasers find it hard to say no because they lack self-confidence. And while many believe that their people-pleasing behaviour will enable them to form healthier relationships, there is no evidence to support this. In fact, by trying to constantly please people you are actually more likely to harm a relationship, as, ultimately, you are going to end up feeling used – even victimised – and resentful of the other person in the relationship, whether they are a partner, a friend or a workmate.[10]

As we have seen, the problem is that a desire to constantly please suppresses negative feelings such as resentment and anger, and if we don't express these feelings in a healthy way, they will, at some point, turn into passive aggression. This means that they will manifest as sarcastic comments, hurtful jokes or even subtle actions, for example, doing someone a favour but not doing it properly, in order to cause annoyance.

In fact, resentment can have a really detrimental impact on relationships, and communicating your feelings is the only way to avoid this happening. After all, if you don't express your feelings, how can the people around you know that you are unhappy? Speaking up for yourself gives people the chance to know when they have done something that bothers you and you can then work together to resolve the issue.

One of the things that I do in my clinic with people-pleasers is role-playing exercises, so that they can practise asserting themselves. Try this with a friend – at first the thought of asserting yourself or saying no will feel foreign, but eventually, if you practise saying no to unfair demands enough, it will start to feel natural.

Fear of Failure

As women, we tend to fear failure, in particular in the workplace, more than our male counterparts. This tendency was highlighted by the Global Entrepreneurship Monitor (GEM) 2012 *Women's Report*, which looked at female entrepreneurship in sixty-seven different countries around the world.[11] The report found that in every one of those countries, women are more scared of failure than men. (Interestingly, this fear was found to be highest in some of the more developed regions that were studied, including regions in Europe, Asia and Israel.)

There are several reasons why many women have such a fear of failure, including the notion that we need to do everything perfectly. Many of us believe that we need to do everything twice as well as men because that's what the women before us did – the ones who broke through glass ceilings and fought for us to have all the opportunities that we have today. But this pressure to prove ourselves can actually prevent us from taking risks and embracing challenges and, at its worst, can become debilitating. The GEM report suggests that women's fear of failure is linked to lower rates of female entrepreneurship around the world (in sixty of the sixty-seven countries in the study, women entrepreneurs were found to be in the minority). This is most likely down to the risk involved in starting a business because, as we saw earlier in the chapter (and in Chapter 3), women are generally less likely to take risks than men.

What's more, sadly, instead of learning from failure, women tend to fear that it's permanent – that a failure is definitive and defining. But the truth is, most successful women (and men, for that matter) do experience failure. In fact, failure is an integral part of the road to success, and if more of us talked about it, maybe we would see it as such. Instead, we are conditioned to try and hide it, which is perhaps part of our people-pleasing nature; we feel constantly under pressure not to let anyone down and not to tell anyone that we are doing anything wrong or that we are less than perfect.

Ambition and Success

'I normally get up an hour early as it takes me a while to blow-dry and straighten my hair and apply my makeup. One morning I overslept and didn't have time to put on makeup or straighten my hair. I walked into my office and felt like everyone was staring at me. I kept my head down. I realised just how much of a difference it makes. Men get away

with so much. No wonder women don't want to
put up with it and throw the towel in early.'

Clara, aged twenty-seven

Although women do, of course, have ambitions, they are
not seen to be as avidly ambitious as men. In fact, there is
often the notion that ambition is a more desirable attribute
in men than it is in women.[12] Because men are so often validated for their work and success, the fact that they are
willing to be single-minded about what they want is seen as
an asset. In the case of women, who are validated for youth,
beauty, motherhood and multitasking, the fact that they
could be ambitious and goal-orientated in that way doesn't
seem to sit as well.

Being told they are ambitious – 'You know, all elbows', as
a student of mine said to me recently – can be seen as an
insult for women, and a trait that may hinder, rather than
help, their climb up the career ladder. By contrast, men seem
to become *more* popular the higher they climb up the professional ladder, as Facebook's COO Sheryl Sandberg points
out in *Lean In: Women, Work, and the Will to Lead*.[13] She says:
'Success and likeability are positively correlated for men and
negatively for women. When a man is successful, he is liked
by both men and women. When a woman is successful,
people of both genders like her less.' Sandberg believes that
women are actually taught to steer clear of power, and in
doing this they limit their ambitions and potential for success.

Most of us would agree that success requires change – you

are unlikely to achieve great success if you are unwilling to adapt. But change can have both positive and negative consequences and often, while someone may claim to want to succeed at something, the reality is that the negatives outweigh the positives for them.

Another reason why we may be reluctant to work towards a goal and strive for success is that, as we have already seen, women are socialised at an early age to be empathetic towards others. We are raised to consider other people's feelings before we even begin to address our own personal desires. This could mean that we might be reluctant to do something for fear that our actions may have repercussions for someone else. For example, we may resist working towards a promotion because we're worried about offending someone else who has hopes of being promoted; or we may worry that we are taking away from someone else's capabilities and achievements (all of this together with the fact that women do not generally want to boast or promote themselves). Alternatively, we may simply feel that we don't deserve the success we've achieved for ourselves.

The notion that women actually fear success was evaluated in a study which found that female college students equated success with a loss of femininity.[14] Another study noted that the female need to conform, to please and to live up to expectations negatively impacted upon women's performance.[15] For example, being accepted into a university that your friends didn't get into – even if it is considered to be better and will most likely mean you achieve more – might make you worry that it will lead to disapproval and rejection from your friends. So you might end up limiting your chances of academic success by going to a lesser university, simply through fear of what your friends might think.[16]

The belief that we are undeserving of success can be directly related to our confidence levels. As women, we often don't want to take credit for something, and we tend not to go after something if we don't feel worthy of it. Comparatively, men are generally more willing to push boundaries and take chances, enjoying the satisfaction that they get from receiving attention.

When you also take into account that women have been found to be behind men in financial literacy, i.e. the ability to understand how money operates in the world,[17] it's hardly surprising that women don't tend to push for better wages. As a result, we can miss out on opportunities, promotions and big pay rises, and this, in turn, means many women get stuck in unfulfilling jobs.

In the workplace, women who *are* determined to gain recognition for their efforts, and who are willing to compete against others, risk placing their gender under attack, with people doubting their success. And at the extreme end of the scale, these determined women can even be seen as taking jobs away from their male counterparts. As a result, they may find that people portray them as unattractive and asexual, calling their sexuality and family life into question; or they may find themselves portrayed as promiscuous and seductive (we've all heard comments like, 'She must have slept her way to the top'). So the resulting fear of appearing ambitious or successful is interconnected with that of not belonging, as women seek acknowledgement and acceptance from their peer group in order to reinforce their confidence.

It is perhaps no surprise, then, that research shows girls perform better when they are in an all-female environment, as we saw in the previous chapter (see page 73). This may be because they feel more able to actively participate in discussions and debates, to take risks and assume leadership positions, when they have no fear of being embarrassed in front of the boys.

Also, a study in 2004 found that teachers in co-ed schools give boys more attention and encouragement than girls in relation to building self-esteem, for example by urging boys to give their opinions or answer questions in class.[18] As a result, girls might underestimate their academic abilities and find it difficult to demand the support and attention they require. This could go some way in explaining why women tend to be more approval-seeking than men, and why we tend to change our behaviour and attitudes around them.

The Inner Critic

Being judged is something that most of us find difficult, as it has the power to impact our confidence, making it hard for us to move forward. This comes down to a lack of self-assurance in our own capabilities and may help to explain why the percentage of women starting their own businesses is low in comparison to men. As we saw earlier (pages 95–6), the 2012 GEM report found that there are significantly fewer female than male entrepreneurs in countries all around the world, and studies suggest that in the UK 11 per cent of women aged between eighteen and thirty start their own businesses, compared to 19 per cent of young men.[19]

The GEM report suggests that one reason for this lack of female entrepreneurs could be the fact that women often underestimate their skills and don't believe that they have what it takes to start their own business. What's more, many women attribute failures to themselves before they have even been judged by someone else, assuming that others will think negatively about them, thus presenting themselves as vulnerable. And this fear of judgement doesn't only apply to the workplace, but can also come into play in many other situations, such as when a woman is revealing something personal, having to ask for assistance or stepping outside of her comfort zone.

In contemporary society many fathers transfer to their daughters the expectations of achievement that men, at one time, only impressed upon their sons.[20] And from an early age girls carry the additional burden of having to conform to cultural ideals of beauty inherited from their mothers – something that boys need not worry about in the same way. In their book *The Triple Bind*, Stephen Hinshaw and Rachel Kranz explore the negative implications of these social pressures on young women who find themselves under pressure from both their parents as well as their peers as they grow up.[21] Starting university, for example, can cause high levels of stress in young women, who might be unsure what to expect and are suddenly faced with an overwhelming workload and demanding academic standards. They are expected to be top of their class and achieve outstanding grades, be competitive in sport and make it on to the university teams, involve themselves in extra-curricular activities, work part-time, have a steady relationship . . .

Ultimately, as the saying goes, girls are expected to 'look like a girl, act like a lady, think like a man, work like a boss'. So women may be seen competing like men in institutions that were once dominated by males. But unlike the men, they are doing all of this while attempting to uphold all that is traditionally expected of them as females: pleasing and deferring to others, being nurturing and empathetic and so on.[22]

Kranz and Hinshaw highlight the fact that what was meant to liberate and provide freedom to young women in granting them new opportunities has effectively subjected them to expectations and pressures that can lead to mental and emotional problems such as low self-esteem, anxiety, depression and self-harm. And, sadly, such problems are by no means uncommon. According to the Office for National Statistics, depression is now the most common mental-health problem in the UK, affecting one in five adults. Mental-health problems for British girls aged between five and ten years old is 5.9 per cent, rising to 9.65 per cent for girls aged eleven to fifteen, while in the US 20 per cent of girls between the ages of ten and nineteen experience some form of depression.[23] As a result, many young girls and women become reliant upon prescription drugs such as anti-depressants and sleeping tablets to cope with the everyday pressures that they face.

So Now What?

Combating people-pleasing behaviours and guilt and learning to say no are all about finding a balance. You don't need to stop being who you are – many of your traits, such as friendliness and sensitivity, are extremely valuable and you should hold on to them and be proud of them. But what you *do* need to do is clarify what your own needs are and start verbalising them and asserting yourself. Learn to ask for what *you* want – it's always going to be easier to go with the flow, but sometimes it's good for your self-esteem to be the one who speaks up, the one who chooses the film you'll see at the cinema or the hotel you'll stay in on holiday.

It's also helpful to think about what your people-pleasing triggers are. When you find yourself unable to say no, are you trying to please people out of fear or do you genuinely want to make a connection? This is a vital distinction. If you are afraid, examine your fears. Are they realistic? Perhaps you are afraid of rejection because you see love as conditional or you're worried about betrayal because a friend or partner left you in the past after a disagreement. Whatever is making you feel scared, try to ensure that your anxieties have a basis in reality and are not just a product of unresolved baggage.

Remember, too, that any kind of relationship should be a two-way street: if you find that you are always the one offering rather than asking for help, step back and take a long, hard look at the relationship in question. Fearing that you may disappoint someone is one thing, but fearing that that person will hate you and never talk to you again because you said no or can't help out every time they ask ... well, frankly, if asserting your needs has that effect on someone, it is probably better that they are not in your life. Try to protect yourself from users and manipulators. People around you may have grown used to your people-pleasing nature, but ask yourself this: if someone can't accept that you have your own needs, is it really worth having them in your life?

It's also important to be aware of your behaviour and to take responsibility for how you let other people treat you. Evaluate your boundaries – make sure that there is a balance between what you expect from others and what you expect from yourself. Think about times when you've tolerated or accepted things that seemed intolerable or unacceptable, and what it feels like to be treated with respect by others – and to respect yourself.

Learning to assert yourself and say no to people isn't easy, but there are some simple tactics you can employ to help you. Before you respond to a request from someone, think properly about what you would be saying yes to – what it means practically in terms of time and effort, how other activities and commitments in your life might suffer as a result and so on. Remember that it is your *choice* to say no if you want to. You have your reasons that are meaningful to you and if others aren't happy with that, then so what? It's important to accept that you can't please all of the people all of the time. You need to learn to tolerate the idea of people not being happy with your decisions – real friendships and even healthy working relationships can survive a few nos!

Basing your self-worth on how much you do for other

people is another thing that needs to stop. It's great to help others, but you should do it because you *want* to, not because you feel you *have* to. The acid test should be when you ask yourself the question: 'Am I acting out of choice in doing this or because I'd feel guilty/bad if I didn't?'

If you find it too hard to say no immediately, then learn how to stall – say you'll think about it or ask for some time before you make your decision. And when you do say no, make sure you *mean* no. Don't let others grind you down – stick to your guns! This doesn't have to mean being rude or aggressive – in fact, it means communicating more effectively. Listen to the other person's needs and then relay your own.

Lastly, if you do find yourself feeling guilty, be clear about what it is you're feeling guilty about. Accept that some things in life you can control and others you can't, so make sure you're not feeling guilty about something that is out of your control. And remember that *feeling* guilty doesn't *make* you guilty. Guilt often comes from judging yourself by impossible standards – so don't feel guilty about not being perfect because there is no such thing!

CHAPTER 5

•

Super-sexualise Me

'It feels like the only thing that matters is how attractive a guy finds you – all that "It's what's on the inside that matters" stuff is a lie. What matters is not how kind or smart or creative you are – what matters is "Are you sexy?" and "Can you get a guy to want you?" I hate that I have to think about how attractive I am to men to feel good about myself but I do.'

Cassie, aged twenty-four

A basic tenet of a psychological model called Social Learning Theory is that people learn through observation and that they are likely to imitate those behaviours that they see as being valued or rewarded. With that in mind, let's consider exactly what both men and women have been 'observing' in terms of sex and sexuality in our culture over recent years.

The world is saturated by more images today than at any other time in our modern history, but what is really important are the messages behind these images. Underlying every picture are value judgements, guides and expectations about who we should be and how we should behave. The predominant message that is perpetuated to girls is that their value depends on their desirability and to boys that they need to be hypermasculine, strong and in control. As mentioned in Chapter 2, sexualised images have featured in advertising since mass media first emerged. What is different now, however, is the unprecedented rise in both the volume and the extent to which these images are impinging on everyday life. This is, of course, largely to do with technology: in the 1970s we were viewing on average five-hundred ads per day, whereas now it is estimated that we are exposed to around five thousand.[1] Kids and adults alike are spending longer hooked up to devices, and because there is so much more media and so much more noise for advertisers to cut through, they are pushing boundaries and becoming more extreme in how they try to get our attention.

One of the biggest issues facing gender equality is the utter inequity between the way that men and women are portrayed in the media. The female body is so often objectified in advertising and pop culture that it sends the insidious message to both men and women that consuming and commodifying the female form is absolutely normal. Let's just take a minute here to think about the word 'objectification'. Its root is the word 'object'. An object is something that is acted upon – you do things *to* objects. A subject on the other hand is the doer, the one who is doing things to the object; so the object is passive while the subject is active. In today's society women's bodies are objectified far more commonly than are men's. In fact, 96 per cent of all sexualising imagery is of women's bodies.[2]

And to be clear, sexualisation is not the same as being sexy – it is the term used to describe the use of sexual attributes as a measure of an individual's value and worth in society. Having sexual feelings, feeling sexy, enjoying sex, experimenting with it – these are all normal, wonderful parts of life. What I'm talking about is the constant, contrived portrayal of women's bodies (or parts of them), routinely and to the exclusion of any other human characteristics, as sex objects for the pleasure of others.

And it's everywhere. Objectification is in the music videos that use women as decorative objects in the background, it's in the commercials that find a way to incorporate breasts into campaigns for everything from shoes to cars to burger restaurants. It's in the fact that it's normal for men to whistle at women as they walk down the street, but not vice versa. It's in the way that most men's and women's magazines feature the same female body type on their covers. It's in the difference between Halloween costumes for boys (scary) and those for girls (sexy). It's in the fact that breast implants have overtaken nose jobs as the most common cosmetic surgery procedure for young women. And it's in article after article telling us how to adapt our bodies and behaviours to be more desirable. And therein lies the problem: because it really is everywhere and because it is relentless, the objectification of women has become normalised; it feels like that's how it's supposed to be, so that things that should incense us, that should make us stand up and shout 'WTF!' simply go unnoticed or remain unchallenged.

As images that would have been found shocking just a few years ago flood the mainstream, so the boundaries are pushed further and further. We are now seeing adverts that reference gang rape or in which women are reduced to dismembered body parts. In fact, the influences of the iconic visual constructs of porn are contributing to the emergence of a caricature of what it means to be a woman. Being beautiful, being attractive, being sexy is no longer about individuality and the characteristics that make a person unique; it's about ticking boxes on a checklist: big breasts, big lips, fake hair, fake nails and so on.[3]

A perceptive point expressed in an article examining sexual portrayal put it like this:

> ... the message from advertisers and the mass media to girls (as eventual women) is they should always be sexually available, always have sex on their minds, be willing to be dominated and eventually sexually aggressed against.[4]

We teach boys from a young age that it's OK to consume women's bodies. And, at the same time, we teach girls that being valued and validated for their sexual desirability above all other attributes is something to strive for. So as we grow up we accept that male sexuality should be more active, as opposed to passive, and that men using women is normal. Men don't need to look a particular way to be taken seriously. We don't see men's underwear advertised with close-ups of testicles and slogans shouting 'Hello Girls!'; men's bodies aren't dismembered to get us to buy random products; men don't dance around semi-naked in music videos while women play instruments and sing fully clothed. Men are seen as whole human beings – not an amalgam of various sexual parts – and because there is less of a focus on how they look, they can spend less time self-objectifying or worrying about their appearance and instead focus on their goals and careers. As mentioned in previous chapters (see pages 34 and 73), psychologists believe that this kind of self-objectification is the reason why girls take fewer STEM subjects (science, technology, engineering and maths) in school and why they have less political efficacy; it is also a core contributor to eating and body-image disorders and a reason why women engage in body monitoring significantly more than the average male. Put simply, objectification actually begins to minimise women's contribution to and efficacy in society.

In her TED talk on the subject in 2013, feminist and political scientist Caroline Heldman[5] described a test she developed – the 'sex object test' – to assess whether or not images were objectifying. An image is objectifying, she says, if:

- it shows only parts of a sexualised person's body – or a part stands in for the whole (an example of this would be an advert depicting a woman's torso emblazoned with a beer logo – she is, in effect, decapitated – so depicting her as a sexy bottle)
- it presents a sexualised person as a stand-in for an object (Roman Abramovich's fiancée, for example, caused an uproar using a black model as a chair for one of her fashion shoots)

- it shows a sexualised image as interchangeable – as one of many items that can be swapped (for example, one advert depicted a man selecting a girl from a 'girl' vending machine)
- it affirms the idea of violating the bodily integrity of a sexualised person who can't consent (lots of famous fashion ads depict glamourised rape scenes in which several men dominate/subjugate female models)
- it suggests sexual availability, as if this is the person's defining characteristic (Heldman gives the example of an advert for pre-owned vehicles in which a woman is looking into the camera seductively and the caption reads: 'You know you are not her first but do you really care?')
- it shows a person as a commodity to be bought and sold (an example of this is a fashion-house advert showing the model posed as a Barbie doll in a box, complete with rigid limbs, vacant eyes and accessories to dress her in)
- it uses the body as a canvas (such as adverts in which women's bodies are written on, as though they are billboards).

Given these guidelines you'd be hard pressed to argue that there isn't disproportionate media objectification of women. But the problem is that these messages filter into our sub-conscious and they affect the way that we see sex and sexuality and our role within them.

Sticking to the Script

In the twenty years from 1979 to 1999 the advertising spend worldwide increased from $20 billion to $180 billion,[6] and stands today at an estimated $467 billion.[7] And the reason why people spend so much on it is because, simply stated, advertising works. It affects our attitudes and our attitudes, in turn, affect our behaviour. Advertising teaches us from a very early age what society values and what we should aspire to. It tells us that sex sells – but if that's the case, why is it that we don't see semi-naked, sexy men plastered all over billboards and commercials? Is it perhaps not so much that sex sells, but rather that those producing these images are making assumptions about what we want to see? It seems to me to be similar to the thinking that guides decision-making in Hollywood – namely that women will watch stories about men, but that men aren't interested in stories about women. Media creates consciousness, and if those creating it are so biased as to assume that the heterosexual male gaze is the only one that matters, then we need to ask ourselves if it's time we stopped buying into what they are trying to sell us.

I have done a lot of work over the years on the effects of sexualisation on kids and teens, but I have no doubt that it affects young adults as well. In my clinics I often see beautiful young women trying to make sense of how their partners can be so out of tune with their needs when it comes to sex. One told me recently:

'I really like him, but he likes it really rough – he likes to pull my hair and sometimes talks dirty, calling me names, but just when we're in bed. I pretend I'm OK with it because he obviously likes that, but I'm not really.'

Soraya, aged twenty-six

This idea – that women feel that they have less volition over what they can demand from their sexual experiences – is something that I am coming across more and more often. Another woman told me:

'I think there is an expectation that if you aren't open to everything in bed, then somehow you are not open-minded – you aren't cool or comfortable with sex . . . and, of course, you feel that if you won't do something, he'll just find someone else who will, so the pressure to please him so that he won't leave is kind of always hanging over you.'

Tanya, aged twenty-one

There has been a shift from the mutuality of the sexual experience, such that women now feel that the way to show their sexual prowess is by being the best at satisfying their partner, sometimes to the detriment of what they enjoy or feel comfortable with. Both in my research and my clinical work I come across young women – even girls – who have been duped into the idea that sexual empowerment means giving the best oral sex, regardless of whether or not they derive any pleasure from it, or whether it is reciprocated, so that they can gain sexual pleasure from the experience as well. Far too often it's about not deviating from the script, irrespective of what it is that we really want.

There has been such a focus on portraying women in terms of what they can offer up sexually to please their partners that this now seems to be the end goal, with little attention paid to what we want or what we feel is good for us. The whole 'faux lesbian' trend is, to a large extent, a product of this: while the LGBT movement has fought against bigotry and misunderstanding for years, the fact that straight women are simulating lesbian relationships in order to titillate men is another example of how little ownership and volition we have over sexuality. Again, it boils down to 'I must make you desire me' as opposed to 'This is what I desire'. Now obviously making someone want you is an important part of sex and relationships, but the point is that, once again, we are working to a script here – and one that is handed down to us by marketeers, pornographers and a celeb culture. And isn't it interesting that we don't see men on TV talking about that one-off experiment with another guy back in college, declaring themselves bicurious in interviews or singing about kissing cherry-ChapStick-flavoured boys and liking it? And why not? Well, again, it goes back to marketing – and at the moment faux lesbianism is predominantly done for and by heterosexual men who see it as a cool selling tool.

And then, of course, there is the question of mixed messages. It's ironic that despite all the gratuitous sexualisation of women, there is still this ridiculous idea in our society that men are supposed to have a lot of sex and that women aren't.

Studies show that one of the dilemmas that faces young women is wanting to attract the male gaze, while at the same time trying to determine what is considered crossing the line of acceptability and going 'too far'? Experimenting with certain types of sexual behaviour for a young woman is often labelled 'unhealthy and immoral',[8] and having a lot of partners or a more relaxed approach to sex can lead to her being identified as a sexual object, rather than a potential relationship partner – something that men don't have to contend with in the same way.[9] That's not to say, of course, that this type of polarisation of the sexes and gender stereo-typing doesn't also have a negative impact on men, who often feel like they are failing if they don't sleep with enough women to keep up with the hypermasculine ideals that are also valued in our society.

Sex versus Porn

I remember when we were first given our biology textbooks in secondary school how everyone was giggling nervously while trying to locate the clinical diagrams of genitalia. Those black and white illustrations were fascinating for a bunch of eleven- and twelve-year-olds who were trying to make sense of the new and exciting world of sex that was unfolding before them. I also remember my friend finding a VHS tape of a porn movie in her brother's sock drawer a few years later and how we sneakily tried to watch it on her old

TV, which distorted colours so badly that for a long time afterwards we were both convinced that certain bodily fluids where a light shade of blue!

Anyway, bodily fluid tones aside, my point is that wanting to know about sex and trying to get as much information as we can about it is a normal, exciting part of growing up. And while textbook illustrations of genitalia and fuzzy *Playboy* movies have always been around in one guise or another, there is something both quantitatively and qualitatively different about what we are seeing today when it comes to porn.

Porn sites make up around 1.5 per cent of all websites[10] and several of them are among the most viewed sites in the UK. In fact, each day search engines deal with something like 68 million requests for pornographic material – that's around a quarter of all searches on the net.[11] So we know we are seeing a lot more of it, but unlike the one-guy-one-girl, 'Hey-baby-did-you-order-a-pizza?' kind of porn that was around a few years ago, today's pornography is different. The trend for 'explicit', 'hardcore' and so-called 'gonzo' porn depicts sex free from any pretence of narrative or relationships and often shows one woman being handled roughly, called names and pushed to her physical limits by several men.

Given how accessible pornography is, and how frequently its themes (from shaved pubic hair to fake boobs) are found in popular culture, it's important to think about how it affects our behaviour. As discussed earlier, according to Social Learning Theory, people learn through observation, and behaviours that are rewarded are likely to be imitated.[12]

But what is important to note here is that it is not necessarily the actual content of the media that has the biggest impact, but the implicit values that it represents. So what we are being affected by is not the image of two people having sex, but the nuances around how they are behaving towards each other, their attitudes and how they relate to each other. So if what we see is a woman refusing a guy's dominant, rough sexual advances, but eventually giving in and getting pleasure from them, the message is that if you're rough enough, even if she initially says no, don't listen because, eventually, both you and she will enjoy it.[13]

Of course, as is the case with all media, the effect it has on us is mediated by the image's or narrative's perceived realism and the way we engage with it. But it should be noted that many studies have demonstrated that the pairing of sexual arousal and violence results in more misogynistic attitudes than viewing sexual explicitness or even non-sexualised violence against women alone.[14]

So what do the 'scripts' that we get from porn convey to us? They highlight the idea that men need to be sexually dominant and insatiable; they emphasise unrealistic beauty standards and the notion that sex is uniformly about penetration – a physical act devoid of any other human connection; they tell us that women generally love being ejaculated on, happily blinking out semen from their eyes; and they show that concepts like cuddling and foreplay aren't really relevant.[15]

Yet these 'scripts' don't reflect the truth of what sex is like in real life. Yes, sometimes a hot, steamy, purely physical relationship is great, but other times it is about foreplay or emotional intimacy. Sometimes it's about being too tired or finding it hard to get in the mood because we can't get over a comment that hurt our feelings – or any one of a million different things that the unrealistic portrayals of sex in most porn do not depict. And while all these things no doubt contribute to our general confusion as to what it means to be sexy and satisfy ourselves and our partner, the most worrying aspect is the inequality and violence that underlie so much of modern pornography; in fact, a content analysis of the fifty bestselling porn movies found that subjugation and aggression were the dominating themes throughout: 50 per cent of over 300 scenes reviewed contained verbal aggression and over 88 per cent contained physical aggression, 87 per cent of which was committed against women. But most concerning was the fact that 95 per cent of the women's responses either displayed pleasure or seemed neutral.[16]

Perhaps the biggest irony of all is that high sexual objectification actually makes sex less fun, decreasing enjoyment of it and possibly even leading to sexual dysfunction, because we become so fixated on ensuring that we look good during sex that instead of being in the moment and really enjoying it, we worry about how we look, how we're measuring up. It's as if we are standing outside of our bodies and judging ourselves. Good sex is not a performance; you don't need to look a certain way or feel you have to direct your own mini porn flick in your head. It's something that you can do literally with your eyes closed, and the trick is being present in the moment – focusing on how it feels and having a sense of entitlement, so you are able to ask for what you want and say no to what you don't want, while affording your partner the same respect. Genuine intimacy, whether it's with a one-night stand or a long-term partner, comes from having the self-respect and self-knowledge to allow another person close to you.

From Sexualisation and Objectification to Violence

Taken to their most disturbing conclusion, the sexualisation and objectification of women contribute to a culture in which sexual violence is not taken seriously. And one of the most damaging and insidious consequences of this is that it reinforces the idea that male power over women is normal. It underscores gender inequality and promotes the message that women are submissive, that they should want to be wanted and that they should even see harassment as a compliment. Of course, there is nothing wrong with experiencing desire for someone – for wanting someone to be attracted to you. The difference here is that through objectification a person's thoughts, feelings and even their identity are ignored and whether they want the attention or not becomes irrelevant – all that matters is that they are sexy and, ultimately, they are assumed to want the attention. With women constantly portrayed in this hypersexualised way, people are led to believe that *all* women fit this one basic stereotype and that it is, therefore, OK to relate to them all in the same way.

In a world where women's bodies are routinely turned

into 'things', we normalise the idea that they are there to be used, as are other objects. In fact, dehumanising of any kind – including racism or homophobia – makes justification of violence easier.[17]

These messages can also potentially harm young men, who are pressurised to act out a version of 'being a man' in which power over women is normal. Research findings show that people viewing sexually objectifying images of women in mainstream media are more likely to be accepting of violence because of the tendency to see women as objects and the recognition of aggressive attitudes and behaviour as the norm. So both the images we consume and the way we consume them lend credence to the idea that women are there to be used and that men are there to use them.[18]

Love – On Demand?

'I was recently talking with girlfriends about how the move into online dating [particularly with apps like Tinder/OkCupid] is further encouraging the notion that women are disposable objects for men: the next person is so readily available that it is easy to lose all sense of manners when dating, as men are just a swipe away from someone who could potentially be prettier or skinnier – particularly with apps that encourage photographs rather than information or details, so you are forced to decide whether someone is a "match" purely on their *looks. Because there is so much emphasis on looks, women feel the need to include selfies or bikini shots as it raises their chances of a match, rather than the fun pictures that men have that show their personality!'*

Keira, aged twenty-five

Sex and love are timeless concepts and, as such, remain pretty static – at least in the abstract. What does change is the way that we engage with and pursue them because of changes not only to do with social politics and cultural norms, but also to do with economic and technological advances. No longer do we need to go to a club or even a friend's house to meet someone; in fact, no longer is it necessary to come up with a pick-up line (at least not right away) – there's an app for that now.

Brands like Match.com and OkCupid – the more traditional online matchmakers – have apps that give you access to how you are faring in the online dating world, wherever you are. Then there is Chatroulette, which pairs you randomly with people from around the world – perhaps not particularly conducive to traditional romance, but great if you're up for the thrill of meeting someone new or glimpsing the odd exhibitionist flashing his groin at his laptop. And then there are apps like Grinder that are perhaps less about finding 'the one' and more about finding 'the one nearest you', as proximity rather than compatibility is the goal. There are also the hot-or-not type of apps like Let's Date and Tinder and 'concierge' dating apps like Grouper –

each trying to find the next iteration of the mating dance. With the success of applications like these, it seems we have become so used to our 'on-demand' culture, which allows us to access products and services quickly and easily, that we are now applying the same principle to relationships. The need for instant gratification makes sense if we're talking about a hook-up, but will it impact on what some would argue is an evolutionary need for genuine human connection?

There is no doubt that technology affects how we evolve socially, whether you accept arguments from people like American author Nicholas Carr, who blames the Web for growing cognitive problems, or you are more likely to side with the views of journalist and writer Clive Thompson, who believes that new technologies are actually enhancing our abilities.[19] From biochemical changes in our brains to adapting our thumb-to-mid-finger gait (to fit the shape of our smartphones) our choices, in terms of what we consume and how we engage with the technologies around us, affect who we become, both as individuals and as a society. But unlike biological evolution that is about the adaptive traits that aid our survival, technological evolution is driven by what we want, rather than what will ensure our existence; worse than that, it's often driven by what marketeers tell us will make our lives easier and better.

Some theorists have argued that in the same way that biological atrophy occurs when we don't use a particular body part (think tails and fur), technologies that stop us from using particular social skills may make some of these obsolete.[20] To a large extent the point of new technology is that it's supposed to make life easier, so we can focus on the important stuff; but it may be that in making things too easy it actually ends up eliminating the important stuff.

In his paper on the topic, Tim Wu, a professor at Columbia Law School and the former chair of the media reform group Free Press, makes the point that while we all know that it's easier to drive to the top of a mountain rather than climbing it, the feeling of accomplishment you get from driving up is never the same. I wonder if the same applies to relationships and technology.[21] The idea that we are given all the 'need-to-know' info on a plate, that we can swipe through two-dimensional images that probably don't really capture the essence of who a person is, that we expect each other to distil our identities into catchy sound bites for others to assess and rate – could all this mean that in our quest to make finding a mate easier we are actually selling ourselves short? Are we making it *so* easy that we are going to get to a place where we can't see the point of making the hike to the top of the relationship mountain?

The fact is that when it comes to relationships we are communicating in ways that up until a few years ago we never did – and this has both benefits and drawbacks. So I guess the main point is to make sure you are communicating what you intend to and that the technologies you are using are tools for helping you express yourself, rather than devices that constrict or contort the message that you want to get across.

Digital Footprints

A single friend of mine recently told me: 'Today it's all about texting – in fact, calling someone can seem a bit odd, even needy or in your face.' And it seems that texting – whether it's words or images – does break down inhibitions.

Rihanna has been quoted as saying, 'If you don't send your boyfriend naked pictures, then I feel bad for him.' You have to wonder what kind of an impact a statement like that might have, given our celeb-obsessed culture. But interestingly, once pictures she sent to her boyfriend were leaked to the public she said:

> It was the worst thing that could possibly ever happen to me. I just felt like my whole privacy was taken [away] before [with an earlier photo leak] and then, when that came out, I thought, 'Oh great, so now there's nothing they don't know about me and my private life.' It was humiliating and it was embarrassing – especially my mother having to see that.[22]

However, the message about one's privacy and digital footprint is, sadly, not what was most widely reported at the time. And Rihanna's experience is by no means rare. Some researchers suggest that sexting is one of the biggest sources of porn distribution and this has implications for potential sexual abuse, exploitation, embarrassment and bullying. The findings of a study in 2012 illustrate that sexting appears to be 'an experience that is pressurized yet voluntary –

they choose to participate but they cannot choose to say "no".'[23]

Interestingly, some researchers who have studied women's depictions of themselves in sexts found that the way girls and young women are posing, pouting, dressing and 'styling' their bodies reflects the extent to which the porn industry is influencing behaviour.[24] Others have noted that it's usually a partner who makes the request from the girl for images motivated by sexual pleasure,[25] so leading to pressure to conform. However, as researchers point out, it's often a lose–lose situation, as the girl risks being labelled either as a 'slut' or as 'frigid'.[26] The actual sexts, meanwhile, are validating for the receiver, the images being regarded as 'trophies'[27] or a type of 'commodity or currency' called 'ratings'[28].

Not surprisingly, most of us don't realise that images posted on social networking sites actually become the property of the site in question, in line with the terms and conditions when signing up. An article on Sky News entitled 'Revenge porn: man charged with extortion' described how a man in his late twenties created a website from hacking into other people's sexually explicit photographs and linking it to their personal Facebook pages. He then revealed their names, ages and location and, knowing this would embarrass and humiliate the victims and their families, gave them the opportunity to have the pictures removed by paying hundreds of dollars. Similarly, applications like Snapchat, where you can send contacts and online friends a picture of yourself, giving them up to ten seconds to view the image before it's deleted, may feel safe. However, these images can be 'screenshot' and then spread among the recipient's friends or leaked online. This, of course, as we all know, can lead to bullying, as well as threats and blackmail.[29] And with proliferation comes normalisation, so it is no surprise that when researchers examine the content of people's webpages they find that a lot of them are posting sexually explicit images of themselves on social networking sites and regulating each other with sexist, derogatory and demeaning language.[30]

Sext, Lies and Video Games

And it's not just online technology that has the potential to inform and affect sexual behaviour. Video games are becoming more and more graphic and realistic.[31] In the newest Grand Theft Auto, for example, the player is able to purchase sex from a prostitute, selecting from a drop-down menu the service they would prefer – from $50 for a blow job to $70 for a half and half or $100 for everything. Using their controller they may then position the camera to get a good angle while she screams, 'Oh my God, fuck yeah, give it to me.' Afterwards, they leave her there, running their car over her and/or beating and raping her. Once she is dead the player can take back their money. This is encouraged in the game as the character's life points increase when they have sex with a prostitute.[32] Now, while I'm certainly not suggesting that there is direct causal effect between exposure to these games and behaviour, it is conceivable that what is depicted in terms of the power imbalance and violence against women in realistic gaming environments does have the potential to affect and influence personal attitudes around what is acceptable, as well as cultural norms regarding what, as a society, we deem as entertainment.

So Now What?

How have sex, sexiness and sexualisation gained such favour in recent years as to be the measure by which women's and girls' worth is judged? While it is not a new phenomenon by any means, there is something different about the way it occurs today and how it impacts on younger and younger girls.

Dr Betty McLellan[33]

Over thirty years ago the cultural theorist Marshall McLuhan pointed out that we perceive the media's effect on us about as well as fish perceive the water they swim in. The objectification of women and the hypersexualisation of culture have become so ubiquitous that they are like background noise – always there, but no longer noticeable.

We, as individuals and as a society, need take a critical look at how the media messages we are exposed to affect us. We need to stop consuming damaging materials that impact our self-concepts. The social ideal of beauty so often presented to us is limiting and the message that underlies it is loud and clear: the most important thing that you can do is to be attractive and the best way to achieve that is to be submissive and overtly sexual. For guys, too, the message is straightforward: be hypermasculine, less emotional and consume the female form – because objectifying women makes you more of a man. Of course, we don't internalise these messages overnight. The process is gradual and insidious – it's in kids' dolls dressed to look like strippers; it's in being able to purchase oral sex from a dropdown menu in a video game, then run over the prostitute who provides it; it's in girls being told that female students shouldn't wear clothes to distract boys because it's not fair to them;[34] it's in men of all different body types dating women of just one body type; it's in the vast majority of TV shows and movies. The same message is everywhere, wallpapering our world, and we need to become aware of it. We need to speak up and say that it's not OK that using women's bodies as objects has become normalised; nor is it OK that both men and women see women's bodies as a mish-mash of sexual body parts, yet they see men as whole human beings.[35]

The good news is that when we do take notice we can really make a difference and start to change things. In early 2014, *Seventeen* magazine in the US pledged to stop Photoshopping pictures, following an e-petition on change.org led by eighth-grade student Julia Bluhm, who decided to do something when she realised that too many of her friends in ballet class were complaining about their weight. And in 2013 Sweden introduced cinema ratings for sexist films – the 'A' rating highlighting films that have a shortage of 'female perspectives'. (The guidance system is called the Bechdel test and is named after US feminist Alison Bechdel; it monitors things like whether at least two female characters talk to each other about subjects other than men.)

Meanwhile, in the UK, thanks to the work of campaign group Object, who tackle the objectification of women in the media, the Leveson Inquiry (a judicial public inquiry set up to examine ethics in the media) acknowledged sexism within the press and the need for any new regulating body to have the power to take complaints from representative women's groups.

So we can change things, but it is so, so important that first we become aware of them. When you see something that doesn't feel right, talk about it, tweet about it, write about it – and do this knowing that all of the big changes that have taken place in the world in terms of equality and justice have done so because individuals had the courage and passion to question that which society had decided was normal.

When it comes to enjoying sex we need to own our sexuality – straight, bi, gay, whatever we feel represents us. We need to feel safe and comfortable enough to explore it on our own terms and not based on the messages derived by a society that presents plastic, manufactured and often damaging portrayals of what 'should' turn us on. Let's learn to enjoy sex, not try and put on a performance. So much of our world seems to be set up to conspire to make us feel bad about ourselves, so that even in the most intimate moments it can be easy to forget that the way sex looks isn't important and that the way it feels is. Sex is not about fake tans, inflated boobs and perfect thighs – it's about the genuine enjoyment of feeling close to someone, be it physically, emotionally or both. You need to feel confident about what you bring to the relationship because if you don't, you will accept more and strive for less. Don't be a sexual object. Be active, not passive; have a sense of entitlement over what you do and don't like.

I said this in Chapter 2, but I feel that it's really important to say it again here: see your body for the amazing instrument it is – for the way it allows you to interact with and experience and derive pleasure and knowledge from the world around you. For too long now we have been seeing our bodies as aesthetic works in progress, rather than as functional tools with which we can make the most of the world around us.

You have a choice. Beauty alone is not something that can ever sustain you, but your thoughts, passions and relationships will. So it's time to stop evaluating yourself and other women in terms of desirability and to get down instead to the deeper business of defining the concepts of sexuality and beauty on your own terms.

•

CHAPTER 6

Avoiding the Bully

'At work sometimes I feel excluded from the main group of girls. I'm not sure if they've meant it, but they often make snide comments about what I'm wearing – that I'm brave wearing flat shoes with my size legs – and I never get invited to go for lunch with them. They always Instagram or Facebook their food and tag each other – I feel like I'm being deliberately left out.'

Zoe, aged twenty-seven

Bullying: it's certainly not OK, but we've all experienced it in one of its many guises, be it at the hands of the popular girls at school, a female boss, 'friends' on Facebook, the girls closest to us or even ourselves. From the playground to the boardroom, social hierarchies underpin relationships and, consequently, bullying isn't something that we necessarily outgrow.

According to certain evolutionary theories, bullying can be traced back to our primitive roots when, over 250,000 years ago, our ancestors had to learn how to survive. It was fundamental for women to establish alliances with other women for survival, but they were also prone to competing against each other – in particular for the attention of men – and this made them feel insecure and vulnerable.[1] It therefore made sense to find a way to control and manipulate situations covertly as this gave them the best chance of getting what they wanted, while posing the least risk of danger.

Bullying among girls and women today is often covert too – there's a hidden culture of female aggression. Girls have a variety of tools at their fingertips with which to belittle each other. These include gossiping about one another, deliberate exclusion and going to the extreme of slut-shaming on social networks. And while women tend to use tactics that don't leave any external bruises, anyone who has been bullied will know that the emotional damage is much worse. And this is why I want to take you through the complexities of female relationships – from the social to the professional – to help you understand why women bully each other and how to rise above it.

The Pack Culture

The idea of 'safety in numbers' goes back to when we were living in caves and depended on each other for safety, shelter and support. While our need to be in a group has transcended a physical need and become a more emotional one, for the modern Western woman today, being a loner is, to put it frankly, lonely. This is why our whole life revolves around groups such as our family, our old school friends, pals from college or uni, the girls we do sports with and our group at work. It goes against all of our social instincts and needs to be isolated – we want to be liked and accepted by others. After all, being part of a group makes us feel protected, needed and that we belong.

With this in mind, it comes as no surprise that our desire to be part of a group is pretty powerful. In fact, as social psychologists have continued to prove over the years, this innate yearning is so strong that groups are regularly formed for virtually no reason other than a wish to be part of one!

People will often form groups with only the most arbitrary differences between members and non-members. Known as the 'minimal group paradigm', this phenomenon was originally recognised by British social psychologist Henri Tajfel and his colleagues, who conducted a well-known study with a group of fourteen- and fifteen-year-old boys back in the 1970s. After being asked to express a preference for some paintings (by Klee and Kandinsky), the boys – who didn't know each other – were then told that they belonged either to a 'Klee' or 'Kandinsky' group. (The names given to the groups created the impression that the selection was based on the boys' preferences, but in fact, the grouping was completely randomised.) What transpired was that they began to behave as groups almost immediately, based on practically no reason at all. In the second part of the experiment, the boys were given virtual money to 'distribute' to the members of each group – those who liked

Klee's work and the others who preferred Kandinsky's. The only information they had about the rest of the boys involved in the study was their member number, but this was enough to ensure they favoured their own group every time. While there was nothing for the boys to gain out of looking after their own group, Tajfel believed that people protect 'their own' because being a member helps them to create their own identity.[2]

Identity formation is a core reason why groups appeal to us; by being around others we are able to answer the big question: who am I? And as well as helping us to work out who we are as individuals, they also help us to form a broader social identity – do we want to be the leader of the group or would we prefer being in the background, for example? However, thanks to social media and the 'me' culture that surrounds us, we've stopped worrying so much about the needs of the group and are obsessed instead with ourselves. So while our social identity may be less important now, our need to be part of a group is still very strong.

For a group to have a strong identity and to be powerful (such as 'the popular group' at school), it is totally reliant on its members – they are the building blocks of the group's image and identity. Group members will share common ground, from something as tenuous as each of them owning a Mulberry handbag (which, according to research, represents money, style and success)[3] to all wanting to work in the entertainment industry.

If we want to be part of a friendship group we have to adapt and alter our behaviour to fit in with the group's norms and behavioural parameters. For example, if we join a netball team, we'll want to share their competitive spirit – we wouldn't treat a big match as a joke if the rest of the group were desperate to win. There is a wealth of studies showing that when we are in group situations we try to conform (even if the behaviour is odd or unusual) because we want to fit in. One of the most famous demonstrations of this is in American psychologist Solomon Asch's work on conformity in the 1950s. He asked individuals taking part in a study to join a group with eight others who pretended to be participants (they were actually actors and had been given clear directions from Asch). They were all shown three lines of varying lengths on a screen and then another line as a reference. The group was then asked to identify which two lines were the same in length. Unbeknown to the genuine participants, the rest of the group (the actors) had been instructed to give the wrong answer. Even though the correct answer was obvious, in over half of the trials 50 per cent of the participants gave the same incorrect answer as the rest of their group and only 25 per cent of all participants refused to be swayed.[4]

In 1962 Asch took his experiments a step further. In a TV special called *Face the Rear* he used a hidden camera to film a group of actors in a lift and one participant joining them. The actors had been instructed to turn around with their backs facing the lift doors and then to stand facing the right or left, instead of the usual convention of facing the doors. Each time the participant appeared awkward and confused, but then slowly turned round to face the same way as the group.

So our need to conform trumps everything, from what our eyes tell us to common sense. It is, clearly, a very powerful motivator.

Consider this effect against the backdrop of today's technology, where malicious comments seem to escalate and increase in number. Perhaps some of what we see is the result of people feeling they need to align with or show allegiance to a particular group view, whereas in isolation their comments would be more tempered.

The fact is that not only do we want to join groups, but once we're part of one we want it to feel somehow special or exclusive, so consciously or subconsciously we don't want to let others join the group easily.[5] In fact, from the playground to the office, initiation rites exist, even if they are disguised. These can be anything from having to down pints of snakebite on team socials before you join your university's sports team to demonstrating at a rally before you join a political party.

Groups make us feel secure on many levels, and this has multiple benefits that help form a significant base in our lives that we couldn't achieve on our own. But the security we get from being part of a group and the security of the group itself both rely on a careful balance; the group is fragile because it is totally dependent on people whose moods and actions change all the time. So to get the most out of being in a group we need to ensure that we retain enough individual freedom to think about and assess the group's actions. Without this we risk blindly conforming to behaviours, beliefs and attitudes that can potentially be detrimental to ourselves or those around us.

BFFs

For most of us the first groups we feel a part of, besides our family, are our peer groups at school. These groups are formed around shared interests, whether a love of One Direction or going roller-skating on the weekends. The establishment of a group symbolises an act of togetherness and the qualities a group shares reinforce friendship and validate a sense of belonging and purpose within girls' lives. Group camaraderie also helps girls to understand their own personal identity and develop their own values. Girls also imitate and copy one another across a range of areas. This usually begins in primary school and can include anything from frilly ankle socks to wearing pigtails on Wednesdays or having similar packed lunches.

When girls make the move from primary to secondary school and as adolescence sets in, they rely on their friends more intensely, moving away from playing hopscotch in the playground and on to chatting about less concrete and more abstract emotional issues. The group dynamic centres around verbal bonding and girls engage with each other by talking about their personal experiences, stories, inspirations and desires, as well as sharing how they feel about the way other girls behave. Thus the clique is born.

As groups form at school there is a hierarchy: there are the popular girls, the geeks, the girly girls, the high achievers and the sporty ones. Despite the fact that each group has a specific identity, being accepted into the popular group (the top of the social food chain) is seen as one of the greatest concerns facing children at school. The popular girls' group is formed by either including or excluding individuals based on their level of popularity and what they can bring to the group. Typically, there is one girl who stands out from the rest – she'll take the lead and influence the behaviour and attitudes of the group. She'll decide if they will all be trying a no-carbs diet or if they're going to the under-eighteens event that weekend. She will have a best friend and the pair of them will be attached at the hip. Sound familiar? Thought so.

Being rejected – essentially, bullied – by the popular group often has a negative impact, especially for teens who need to feel part of a group to form an identity and a sense of social safety. Research in this area suggests that bullying is intentional. In 'School Bullying' – a report for the NSPCC in 2010 – Alana James of Goldsmiths, University of London, argues that bullying is a deliberate act and its aim is to hurt the victim and cause harm. When friends playfully tease each other it's innocent, but when the motive for teasing is to upset someone, then it is bullying.[6]

Dan Olweus, a research professor of psychology from Norway, also uses this definition of bullying, calling it an 'aggressive, intentional negative act', and he identified that bullying is repetitive and continues over time.[7] Put simply, bullying is a power dynamic playing out between two people, with one asserting control and power over the other. And as I mentioned earlier, bullying does not have to be physically aggressive, with hair pulling or fist fights; girls predominantly use more covert and damaging tactics towards their victims,[8] bullying more passively than boys.

The type of bullying 'tactics' girls use was highlighted in

a study in which researchers identified calculated techniques such as gossip, rumours, alienation and social exclusion when belittling victims.[9] The bully would convince the others in the group to participate, therefore skilfully sharing accountability for the bullying between them; this not only dilutes responsibility, but makes the rest of the group connect over a shared secret or bad behaviour. Unsurprisingly, this leads to the victim feeling even more violated and isolated.

So, whereas boys are much more physical with their bullying tactics, tending to lash out by hitting or punching each other, and it is likely that the bullying stops there (although it can also extend, via phones or social networks – see page 148), girls do not follow this pattern and it can be easy for their bullying to go unnoticed. A common line used by girls in the playground is 'You can't play with us', and they'll use a similar approach the next day and the day after, so the bullying is ongoing. Women and girls also tend to be more secretive about their bullying. Swedish researchers in the early 1990s looked at female and male aggression and found that women behaved just as antagonistically as men, but only when there was no danger of someone witnessing their behaviour.[10]

This style of covert bullying and aggression has been dubbed 'relational aggression'.[11] After studying how girls form close and affectionate relationships, researchers found that bullies would use this bond against their victims as a way to hurt and emotionally injure them. For example, if three close girlfriends always swapped their Barbies' clothes, but then one girl took the outfit another girl wanted, the bully would then exclude this girl from the group, telling the others that she was always damaging the clothes and that she couldn't play with them any more. This would be a way of using the friendship against the victim. It is control by exclusion and explains why the spreading of rumours to persuade others to reject an individual is so often used as well.

The Popular Girl a.k.a. the Queen Bee

When you think of the popular girl, Regina George of *Mean Girls* probably springs to mind – and real life is no different. The girl who bullies is often the popular girl at school and everyone wants to be part of her group; she's smart, she's in the top team in sports and all the boys fancy her. And it's often the same with grown women who bully too – they're the ringleader in their clique and everyone else wants to fit in with them.

But why do girls bully? The reasons are varied. In some cases they have experienced bullying or abuse at home, and so model the behavior they see in their own family dynamic; in others, the girl who bullies simply enjoys the power and domination – even the attention – she gets from acting out. In either case, bullying behaviour often has to do with an inability or insufficient maturity to cope socially, and lack of empathy is often a defining characteristic.[12]

As we know, however, bullying isn't confined to school-girls; the office is also a common location where women intimidate other women. In fact, 35 per cent of American women admitted they'd been bullied at work, according to a 2010 survey by the Workplace Bullying Institute.[13] Dr Gary Namie, who conducted the study, believes that women often bully female colleagues as a way to progress in male-dominated environments. I always find this notion interesting from a feminist perspective: the idea that gender-stereotypical beliefs about what strength and control look like will dictate workplace behaviour – that morphing into an 'alpha male' is the only way for a woman to get ahead in business.

The bully has unmatchable power socially, being in charge of who is included in and excluded from her group. She takes on an active role in emotional persecution, making comments or jokes about the way other girls or women dress, their weight, the quality of their work, etc. And just like many bullies, she may be insecure herself – scared that her position of power will be taken away from her by someone else or that she'll face competition that will jeopardise her place in the group.

If someone is beautiful, talented and does well at school or work it can make the people around her feel inferior. The bully and her accomplices will justify picking on such a girl because they can label her as full of herself and decide to make her aware of her behaviour – they give themselves the perfect excuse to pick on her and take away any chance that she will become popular herself.

This style of covert bullying actually gains momentum and increases as girls grow up and competition for male attention is fierce.[14] Sociologists Elizabeth Armstrong and Laura Hamilton found that 'mean girls' continue to be bullies at university and later on at work, too. And, as they get older, female bullies become even more subtle with their tactics.[15] In fact, it seems that adult bullies may actually feel better about themselves when they antagonise others, controlling other women by putting them down and exploiting power dynamics.

In any set-up there is only room for one alpha female and once she is in position she won't let anyone get in her way or take her status away from her. In her book *Queen Bees and Wannabes*, author and educator Rosalind Wiseman looks at the power dynamics in female friendship groups. She suggests that there often tends to be a Queen Bee who controls the 'Banker', whose role it is to collect information from the other girls in the group (i.e. gossip) and then distribute it around the group like an infection that spreads and creates conflict.[16] The Queen Bee is skilled enough to distance herself from the rest of the girls sufficiently to prevent them from getting anywhere near her position at the top.

Some would argue that Margaret Thatcher was a prime example of this.[17] The UK's first female prime minister, she wasn't interested in women's issues; instead, her attitude was: 'I made it. Others can jolly well do the same.' Thatcher adopted a masculine, very assertive, controlling style of management, so that she stayed in power and was able to ensure that she was in charge – this is why she was dubbed the 'Iron Lady'. Sadly, a message that has often been perpetuated in the business world is that for women to succeed at work they need behave in the same way as men, i.e. be ruthless. This is often taken to mean that manipulation and bullying other women are OK.[18] So women are encouraged to demoralise each other and eradicate competition – in the same way the popular girl did at school.

In 2012, Professor Michelle Duguid from the Olin Business School carried out a study into why women at the top of the business world were less than willing to encourage and support new up-and-coming, ambitious women.[19] She found three key factors: competitive threat, collective threat and favouritism threat. The competitive threat is quite literal – it means women are worried the newcomer will be more qualified/talented/skilled than they are and will overshadow them. On the flip side is the collective threat, whereby the latest female addition to the office is seen as less qualified than the bully, who worries that the newbie will play up to negative stereotypes of women and affect the status quo for the rest of the women at work. The third factor, the favouritism threat, is – as crazy as it sounds – where women are scared of appearing to support other women.

In the workplace you shouldn't have to positively discriminate. In the same way that you shouldn't hire someone just because they're black or white or Asian, you shouldn't choose a woman just because of her gender. But equally, you shouldn't see other women in the workplace as competition. We've witnessed in banking that the alpha way of working – where only one person was important and made all the decisions – didn't work. In fact, the banks that were left standing after the financial collapse in 2007 were those that had adopted a more collaborative approach.

Of course, it's only natural that in today's fiercely competitive job market you will want to make sure you're OK and that you stand out, but we all need to reframe what success means and work out how to use our own skills to shine, as well as using colleagues as a human resource. Leadership is all about using people to the best of their abilities, not putting them down so that you can be noticed. Teamwork is fundamental to any organisation, so remember to use everyone, including other women, at work.

Conversely, when you are on the receiving end it can feel awful, regardless of your age or who you are, making you feel scared, alone and 'less than'. It's natural to wonder 'Why me?' – you may feel that you are doing something wrong and you may blame yourself. But it's not your fault. What's important is how you deal with it. If it's just a minor annoyance, then ignoring it and not engaging is often the best way forward. On the other hand, if it's something you find yourself thinking about a lot, that is making you feel bad about yourself or affecting your mood, it is important that you do something. Most bullies feed off their victims' reactions, so try not to show fear or upset if possible, but be assertive instead. Try to confront them in a neutral place, think about body language (the way you stand, good eye contact, etc.) and use a confident, non-aggressive tone. Be sure of what you want to say before you say it, stick to the facts and be clear about what you want them to change – the more prescriptive you are, the better. If this doesn't work, you may need to involve a third party – someone from HR, for example, if it's a work situation, or a family member or friend for a domestic or social one. And always remember – when someone is a bully, it says more about them than it does about you.

Bullying in the Mating Game

Bullies are very much an inevitable part of society. Researchers from the University of Ottawa found one reason why women bully each other is to ensure they are at the top of the dating food chain, and they use the techniques of gossiping, criticising appearance, social exclusion and spreading rumours that other girls are sluts to ensure that they stay there.[20]

A staggering number of teen girls have employed these techniques, too. The researchers found that just over half of fifteen-year-old girls studied use bullying or indirect aggression as a way of controlling their peers (as opposed to just one in five boys). We've seen that girls prefer to go about their bullying covertly because unlike beating someone up, there is little chance (if any) that they'll get hurt themselves and they also have the best defence – they can claim they didn't mean to hurt anyone. This type of girl-on-girl aggression tends to get worse as girls grow up and spikes during the teen years and the early twenties, when there's the most competition for boyfriends and sexual partners.[21] It's thought that, as with older women, bullying happens between young women because they're competing for male attention.[22]

If you've been a victim of bullying, it may be of some comfort to you to know that research implies the more attractive you are, the more likely you are to be bullied. It's also been suggested that women who are considered too sexually available or at least more flirtatious and provocative than others are more vulnerable to female hostility. Sex is a powerful negotiating tool for women – it has been since the time when cavemen and -women used it as such in their efforts to attract a partner. Women suppress other women's sexual behaviour by gossiping about them or excluding them, so they improve their own chances of finding a sexual partner. The theory goes that if women are sexually promiscuous, they make sex too readily available and so its bargaining power is devalued, and so other women are unable to use it to negotiate with men. I'm not so sure about the gender bias underpinning this notion, but it is an idea often put forward to explain female bullying from an evolutionary point of view.[23]

With this in mind it makes sense that female bullying is effective – if you put another woman down and make her feel insecure, you make her less desirable and she's no longer a rival for male attention.[24]

The Bully behind a Screen

As we've seen, the digital revolution and endless technological advancements have totally transformed the way we communicate and how we form relationships with each other. It also influences how we bully. Young people in particular are increasingly vulnerable – bullying isn't just happening inside the school walls, it's everywhere, from text messages to online-sharing and social-networking sites.

The power of the internet – where bullies can remain faceless – has made it incredibly difficult for parents, teachers and the police to monitor and control young people's activity online, especially as they are not always *au fait* with the latest apps or technology. And there are so many ways that people can be reached and bullied via social networks, chat rooms, apps, etc. which provide the perfect platform for sexually provocative messages and violent and threatening material. Online – or cyber – bullies also have a variety of ways to cover their tracks.

Cyberbullying, just like online trolling, is a product of the internet and the fact that people can anonymously send messages and spread gossip without the worry that it will be traced back to them. It's not hard to see why it is so appealing. According to a government report on bullying published in March 2013, 38 per cent of young people in the UK have been victims of cyberbullying, and between 2011 and 2012 a staggering 31,599 children called ChildLine to talk about being bullied. To add to these stats, girls are twice as likely as boys to experience ongoing bullying as opposed to a one-off incident.[25]

Technology is taking away the natural stopgaps that allow us to consider what we share before we share it. With the advent of smartphones, film footage can be taken and uploaded to the internet in a matter of seconds. And this is the problem – the instant nature of the online world doesn't allow the space and time for reflection. A few years ago sharing a photo would have involved taking a picture, waiting to have it developed and deciding who to show it to, then either sending it to them or physically meeting up with them. These were all distinct stages of the process and, as such, the decision to proceed or not at any stage would require some thought and consideration. Now you click and you load and, in just moments, a picture can be shared with millions – the implications of which you may not have even have fully considered.

An example of this is the case of the seventeen-year-old 'Slane Girl', famed for her sexual encounters with two men at an Eminem gig near Dublin in 2013. While she was performing oral sex on one of the men, someone took a photograph and by the following afternoon the picture had gone viral. #Slanegirl was trending globally on Twitter and the Slane Girl Facebook page that was set up received eight thousand likes before it was shut down. But by that time the Slane Girl had been identified and her full name published, despite the fact that she was under eighteen. The photos were later removed from the websites and accounts were banned after the girl was called malicious names, including 'slut', 'whore', 'vile' and 'rotten'. While the man involved was dubbed a 'hero' it was later reported that the girl was so badly affected by the ordeal that she'd had to be hospitalised.

Sites such as Facebook allow us to send messages privately or put them on display through status updates, wall posts and photos that the rest of the virtual community can witness and react to. It is also the perfect medium for making people feel excluded: events can be set up and it's easy to deliberately leave someone out and then rub their noses in it by posting lots of pictures and tagging everyone in them. This will then crop up when the excluded person checks their online feed in the morning, only to find they are the only one not to have been invited to someone's party. Such online exclusions or rejections can often spill over into our offline interactions.[26]

The online world is affecting the way we connect with each other on a deeper level, and it is also desensitising us to other people's feelings. We don't fully understand the impact of 'liking' a post or commenting because we are emotionally removed from the side-effects. Acting out online isn't the same as hurting someone in the flesh – you can switch off your phone or iPad afterwards and act as if nothing happened.

Slut-shaming

Social media is causing confusion as to what behaviour is deemed 'normal' online. We are told to be sexually liberated and desirable, but at the same time we need to be innocent. So a selfie profile picture on Facebook has to show us looking hot or sexy, but not like someone who sleeps around. What's more upsetting, as we saw in Chapter 2, is that we seem to be living increasingly with the notion that we should be judged by our sexual appeal. We have to master the juggling act between an online and offline personality and decide what an acceptable sexual identity to express online is.

Because of this we have created a new set of rules for what is considered 'slutty' online and in the real world. Respect from others within our social circle has helped to draw up these parameters. Kissing a friend's boyfriend or posting a topless picture on Instagram, for example, can damage a reputation, and so we have learned to regulate each other's behaviour so as to separate ourselves from the 'sluts' who don't know this key rule[27] – effectively saying, in other words, 'I'm not a slut because I didn't do what this girl did'.

Slut-shaming may be something only young people do, but the victim will continue to be affected when she's much older. Sociologist Michael Flood found that the term 'slut' is a powerful way to regulate women's sexual behaviour, knowledge and expectations.[28]

Being called a slut or having a slutty reputation canhappen to any girl.[29] Behavioural researchers have found that girls become competitive and feel threatened when others are developing faster than they are. If most girls are in crop tops and one girl is wearing a bra it can attract attention from the boys and scrutiny from the girls. The girl with breasts is then vulnerable to being bullied and her body works against her because the bullies spread gossip that she's a slut, despite her not being sexually active.[30] Girls can also be stigmatised for kissing a boy, having casual sex or wearing sexy outfits.[31] And being called a slut isn't just a verbal insult – it has a ripple effect that can lead to harassment, losing friends and being associated with other girls who are notorious for their sex lives, as well as making the victim a more vulnerable target for sexual abuse and bad treatment from boys who think they're 'easy'.[32]

A study in 2011 by Tracy Vaillancourt at the University of Ottawa looked at how people spread sexual rumours and found that women regularly use such tactics in bullying.[33] Young women in the study were put in pairs and teamed with either a beautiful woman dressed sexily or dressed modestly. Every pair aside from two was indirectly aggressive to the sexily dressed woman. What this showed was that sexy women are often seen as a threat by other women, particularly around their husbands and boyfriends.

Psychologist Kathryn Stamoulis believes the term 'slut' is used today in a more 'friendly' way; in signing off texts, for example.[34] She argues that many oppressed groups try to take back control of the word that hurts the most in this way, giving it less power – for example, black people using the N-word. Similarly, after Canadian police officer Michael Sanguinetti suggested 'women should avoid dressing like sluts' to avoid being attacked or raped in 2011, a group of women joined forces to launch feminist protests called SlutWalks in an attempt to highlight the issues around calling women 'sluts'. However, until women's sexuality is seen differently, no matter how much we try to trivialise the word 'slut' it'll still sting in the same way.

When I undertook some research on sexualisation a few years ago it seemed that sexual bullying was on the rise.[35] Whether in the form of online shaming or even physical harassment in schools, colleges or in the workplace, sexual bullying is an incredibly personal attack and can make the victim feel anxious, rejected, depressed and, in extreme cases, suicidal. This, I think, is because we put such a premium on young women's sexual choices and behaviour – in essence, reducing their worth to sexual desirability. We need to stop this – we need to take a stand with regard to the value-laden language we use when talking about women and sex because, ultimately, we are going to end up bullying ourselves for not being able to ascribe to a ridiculous set of poorly set boundaries and antiquated ideals that equate female worth with sexual behaviour.

Frenemies

A frenemy – as well as being a very catchy word that blog-gers love to use – actually holds some merit from a social psychological point of view. Frenemies are passive–aggressive friends who are often competitive; they are happy to be there during the hard times in your life, but struggle to congratu-late you when things are going well. What stings more with a frenemy is that there are plenty of positive things about them and their friendship: they can be amazing friends, but when it comes to men or careers they can be jealous, com-petitive and enjoy putting you down.

What's worse is that this type of relationship is actually bad for your health – research into these 'friendships' shows they can trigger low mood and stress.[36] This was illustrated in a 2003 study where volunteers wore blood-pressure monitors for three days and kept a diary of all social interactions that lasted longer than five minutes, also rating them in terms of quality.[37] As they'd expected, the researchers found that the volunteers' blood pressure went up when they were with ambivalent friends or frenemies. But the surprise result was that the blood pressure was higher around frenemies than classmates or colleagues the volunteers actively disliked!

One reason for this can be that when we don't like some-one there's no surprise element when we see them. Yes, we may feel uncomfortable, but we already know we just don't get along with them. But when it's a frenemy we harbour both hate and love for them – like we would for an ex-boyfriend, perhaps – and so we feel let down by them when they do something to upset us; we don't see it coming.

In an earlier study by the same researchers, 133 people between the ages of thirty and seventy were asked to categorise their friends according to how supportive or upsetting they were.[38] The participants then did two stressful exercises – one was a mental maths task and the other was verbal, where they had to defend themselves against a false accusation. What the researchers found is that the people who had more frenemies in their social circle were more stressed during the tasks – indicated by their increased heart rate and blood pressure. And these people were more likely to show signs of depression, too. So it seems that frenemies can actually add to your stress levels, whereas healthy and supportive friendships help you deal with stress.

With this in mind it seems crazy that we'd have frenemies at all, but studies have shown that we want to hang on to difficult friendships for sentimental reasons, such as having gone to school together. In other words, we'll maintain a relationship with someone because we've known them for so long, despite them not being the best of friends. And we also believe that the positive parts of that person and their friendship outweigh the negative.

If you're intent on keeping your relationship with a frenemy, you need to ensure that where you see a pattern of negative behaviour you have an emotional back-up to support you. So if, for example, this frenemy always cancels on you at the last minute, try not to think it's about you – instead of staying in and feeling low, make other plans with a group of friends and go out with them.

So Now What?

How do we break the apparently endless cycle of bullying?

Firstly, it's important to recognise that it happens to most of us. The word is bandied around a lot these days and it's really vital to separate someone who is teasing you or being rude or annoying, from someone who is victimising you and actively trying to hurt you. In the case of the former, either ignoring the person or speaking to them and giving them some insight into how their behaviour affects you usually does the trick. With the latter, depending on the context (whether it's within the workplace or a social group) it often helps to get a third party involved who can hold the bully accountable. In either case, being able to identify the problem as being in the person who is doing the bullying, as opposed to seeing it as a flaw within yourself, is a good first step.

Some of the worst bullying that I see is the way that we bully ourselves. Good self-esteem comes from gaining a sense of volition over our lives. Focus on and develop your strengths, striving to achieve your goals and accepting recognition for this. Learn and understand what it is that you are good at and capitalise on those talents. And, more importantly, stop bullying yourself by comparing who you are to others; focus on what makes *you* special. Accept that everyone fails at one point or another, but it's how you cope with life's curveballs that matters!

Of course, it can be hard, especially when life knocks you down, but developing a positive attitude and outlook on life is fundamental in avoiding the bully within, as well as those others who try to bully you. To take control and stop bullying in all its forms you need to understand your relationships, be they platonic or sexual. You need to see and value what makes a relationship a healthy one, instead of wishing you were part of the popular group at work or uni or wherever you are. Simply succumbing to what the popular girls do and mimicking how they act/dress/talk can actually result in the opposite of what you want.[39]

It's natural to want to belong to different friendship groups, but when you're with a group of girls at work or want to bond with your new housemates, remember that you shouldn't compromise who you are just to fit in. So if your new housemates want to go to a rave, but you hate the atmosphere and the music, don't go. To get the most out of groups you should make sure you are still an individual with all your own likes and dislikes, as well as a shared life with other people in the group; so you may not want to go to that rave, but you may like going to a cool pop-up bar with your friends instead.

Be aware of the covert tactics women use to bully each other. We are encouraged to put each other down, but don't be the person who does that. Build up your own self-esteem as best you can, so you don't feel the need to look at others and criticise their appearance or their performance at work. And if you are a victim of bullying, remember it's not necessarily because you're seen as weak; very often it's because other women see you as a threat – competition that needs to be eradicated – because you're intelligent and beautiful, so keep telling yourself that!

CHAPTER 7

•

Going It Alone

'I'd always dreamed of working in the entertainment industry and my parents were very supportive. After uni I'd planned to live in London with my best friend in a flat overlooking the Thames. But instead I'm working as an admin assistant for a health centre and live in a house share in a run-down area in the suburbs. I struggle to pay my bills each month and my social life is anything but celebrity-like, even though I wish it was!'

Marissa, aged twenty-four

Remember your career dreams when you were little? Did you want to be a nurse? A ballet dancer? A superhero? When we were children, adult life seemed like just another fun game, although, of course, when we turned into teenagers and experienced our first reality check, realising that we wouldn't look like X (insert name of whichever celeb the media was idolising at the time), we had to accept that life wasn't quite what we imagined it to be.

Unfortunately, we go through the same awakening when we hit our twenties, and I think this is one of the most difficult times for women. It's a transition period when we leave the safety, norms and comfort of home (and our parents) and start life as an independent person. It can also be the era of 'firsts' – first job, first flat share, first move to a new city and first serious relationship – and while this can be exciting, it's also confusing and it's natural to feel insecure about life and wonder, 'Where am I going?'

Because, although Beyoncé may have fired us all up to be independent women, when the bank of Mum and Dad no longer gives handouts and the washing piles up and there are no hugs at the end of a bad day we may not care that we scrimped and saved to buy the Louboutin shoes on our feet – because they hurt a lot, too!

When we take our first tentative steps as adults we have to face the fact that our career, housing and financial aspirations may well fall flat. It's a struggle to survive on a first-job or intern salary, let alone have a wardrobe to rival Victoria Beckham's or a party lifestyle *à la* Kelly Brook. And all the while we're trying to form new friendships and grow our own urban family. It's exhausting – and it's no wonder, then, that it can be a lonely and hard time. But it's something you will learn to manage, I promise.

Miss Independent

What does being an independent woman today actually mean? Well, it can represent a variety of things, from being financially stable to being a single mother. The choices you make define your independence, as well as your financial status – so you can decide whether you want to use credit cards and loans to fund your lifestyle or if you'd prefer to stick to a budget and work extra shifts. If you are living with your boyfriend and paying for half of everything, you can think of yourself as just as independent as the woman who has funded her own trip around the world. So I guess that at its core independence implies autonomy – a sense of self-directedness that allows you to feel you have volition over your own life.

The problem is that when expectations of and a desire for independence aren't met in real life it can be scary, disheartening and even affect the way you see yourself. Society emphasises that by your mid-twenties you should have started off on your chosen career path, be living in a cool part of town and look like a celebrity, the pressure of which can be extremely daunting.

When you leave home for the first time, as exciting as it is in many ways, it can often feel as if the security blanket of your parents has been ripped off and you're left to fend for yourself. The same thing can happen to women who become financially reliant on their boyfriend or husband, then have to start figuring out how to budget for the first time, following a break-up.

People adapt differently to this period in their lives: some feel as if their confidence and sense of security have nose-dived, often because their parents have always stepped in to help, while others relish being self-sufficient and solely in control of everything. Everyone has a different pace when it comes to going it alone and, as with most things, comparing yourself to your friends is not generally the best thing to do. Instead, think about what you are gaining in terms of independence as opposed to what you are losing. So yes, money might be tighter, for example, but there is something quite liberating about prioritising your own needs – it focuses your attention on what's important and even gets you to think about and ask yourself important questions about your values and desires. Remember, there is no power without responsibility, so as daunting as it seems, think about how empowering it is that despite things not being easy, you are managing independently and you are able to trust and rely on your own abilities.

Cash, Careers and Crisis

The economic crisis of the twenty-first century has radically transformed the lives of young people, and not just their immediate futures. The recession that began in 2008 had what some have described as a catastrophic effect on the jobs market and employment prospects, while rents sky-rocketed. In many parts of the UK house prices have risen steeply too, and it is now almost impossible for someone in their twenties to own their own home or put down a deposit, let alone live anywhere near the area they'd like to. And it's no different in the rental market: for someone fresh out of school and about to start university, rent must seem astronomical. In October 2013 the average price of renting a home in England and Wales reached a record high of £757 a month, reflecting an annual rise of 2.1 per cent according to figures from LSL Property Services. Choices are limited: you can either break the bank renting a studio flat or sign up to a house share. But renting is a vicious cycle, the constraints of paying every month meaning it's impossible to save up enough money to buy a property. Teamed with crippling student loans, debts and the high cost of living, owning your own home may well remain a dream.

Employment opportunities drastically reduced during the economic crisis and as companies felt the strain they were forced to squeeze resources and make redundancies or introduce pay freezes. To make life harder, Income Support and Jobseeker's Allowance, as well as many other means-tested benefits, have declined in real terms.

Thanks to the previous Labour government's initiative to focus on 'education, education, education', teenagers since 1997 have been encouraged to continue their education or training beyond the ages of sixteen and eighteen. So the number of people graduating from university took a large hike, rather inconveniently, around the same time as the economic crisis went into full throttle.

This has left the UK with an underemployed, highly qualified workforce. So, having invested many years and even more pounds in your education in the expectation that you would get a good job on completing your studies, you may find you are being exploited in the workforce as you compete fiercely for unpaid or poorly paid internships, and that you have to subsidise any income with other work, rely on your parents for money or move back in with them. And if you are lucky enough to secure work, it may be in a job to which your degree bears no relevance. So it's not unusual to see a biology graduate working as a PA to a director in a property-development company or a history graduate working in logistics.

According to the Office for National Statistics (ONS), the average wage for a woman in the UK in 2013 was around £24,000 a year (or £529 a week), but female graduates were more likely to work in lower-skilled jobs than males. And it doesn't stop there because men also had consistently higher employment rates than women aged over twenty-two. A recent poll of 3600 *Glamour* magazine readers called 'The Mistakes That Girls Make' found that 61 per cent of those who are currently employed spend more than they earn, 38 per cent live off their overdrafts and 46 per cent have no savings to fall back on. According to the ONS, as many as six out of ten young women regularly borrow money from their parents, the average amount for those in their twenties being £103.26 a month. The *Glamour* magazine poll also found that 45 per cent of its readers thought that they would get their dream job in their twenties and 44 per cent wished they had known earlier what they wanted to do – if they had, they thought it may well have been easier to find work as they could have spent their teens doing work experience and gaining a competitive edge.

'My parents were beyond proud when I got a first-class degree, but there was too much competition

*for the jobs I wanted and at twenty-one, I was
claiming Jobseeker's Allowance and living in a box
room with distant relatives. I did occasional night
shifts in a car park, but I've been working in a call
centre for four years and live with five others in a
flat. I could have saved myself the student debt
and just started work at sixteen!'*

Zoe, aged twenty-five

Moving back with Mum and Dad

Rising rent and house prices paired with an unstable job
market and limited opportunities play a fundamental role in
the uncertainty and anxiety you may feel about your life.
Add to this the reality of new places, new friends and a new
life, all balanced against the ideals and values you had
before, and it's no wonder it's so tempting to shun all these
responsibilities and financial independence and return
home to your parents, delaying marriage, children, buying
a house and the many other rites of passage young adulthood brings.

According to the ONS, since 1997 there has been a 20
per cent rise in the number of people aged twenty to thirty
living with their parents, with a third of girls aged twenty
to twenty-four still at home. And with the creature com-
forts already in place it's not hard to see why returning
home – or becoming a 'boomerang kid'[1] – is so appealing.
It offers the freedom to continue studying, save up for a

deposit on a house, buy a new car, save for a trip around the world, start up a 'girl' band or the space to look for the right job without worrying about having to pay bills and rent.[2] Being back home can also offer security, with someone to make your meals, clean the house and wash your clothes.

But as anyone who has moved back home will know first-hand, being a boomerang kid isn't without its catches. As time goes on, it can become difficult living with your parents and, no, I don't just mean stomaching your dad's jokes or the constant feeding from your mum. You may feel that your parents revert back to treating you the same way they did when you were a child; you may have to tell them where you're going and when you'll be back; you may be told to keep your room tidy or asked why you're wearing such a low-cut dress. As you struggle to become independent from your parents despite living with them, it can be a burden (and a headache) constantly to keep them up to date with what you are doing and whether you want dinner – and that's before we get to the endless questions about work, your love life, your finances and everything else. And because you're living under their roof you may feel obliged to report back on every detail of your life; and you may also feel that you don't want your parents to judge you. For example, you might avoid a one-night stand because you know your parents will disapprove.

As time goes on and you begin to change the way you live, you lose not only your independence, but that autonomy that we all crave as part of being happy, well-adjusted adults.

'*After uni I moved back to my parents so I could save up to spend half the year travelling. At first it was great, but then my mum wasn't too impressed with my love of partying and didn't like the fact that I often got home at 3am. So eventually I stopped going out and even decided not to go away and saved for a house instead.*'

Sarah, aged twenty-two

Dating while living under your parents' roof can also be a challenge. Meeting a hot guy on a night out and bringing him back to your parents' can be near impossible. And even though it's harmless fun, you risk being left red-faced or enduring a lecture when you're caught trying to sneak him out the next morning. According to a YouGov survey for the housing charity Shelter in 2012, 50 per cent of young people living at home said it was hard to have a relationship while under their parents' roof. Your parents may have more traditional views than you and may struggle to accept that you are sexually active, even though you passed your sixteenth birthday years ago! While they may be well aware that you're no longer a virgin, it can be hard for your parents to see you in any other way and they don't want to be reminded of that fact when they see a guy leaving your bedroom. So to avoid this awkward moment you'll have to get creative and find different places to be intimate with a partner. You might also find that if you are in a relationship, your parents feel the need to intervene in your arguments, especially if you come home crying, and this can put a strain on your relationship with both them and your partner.

It's hardly surprising, then, that along with the rise in the boomerang effect, the age at which couples decide to get married has also gone up dramatically. In the 1970s the average age for a woman to get married was twenty-one, while in 2000 it was twenty-five (and the same trend can be seen for men too, jumping from an average age of twenty-three to twenty-seven over thirty years).[3]

Figures from the ONS for 2013 found the average age for women to get married is now twenty-nine and for men it's thirty-one. And the age for starting a family has risen too: in 1971 the average age for women giving birth for the first time was twenty to twenty-four, while in 2010 it was thirty to thirty-four, suggesting that the twenties is now a time to focus on career, travel and saving for a mortgage before settling down.

Spoiled for Choice

When the pill became available in 1961 women's lives were transformed: they were able to control when they wanted to have children, as well as how many sexual relationships they wished to have before getting married and, as a consequence, the social stigma of living together and having sex outside of marriage began to erode. Women were no longer restricted to raising a family – they had the option to go to college and university, they could have careers and there was more gender equality at work.

Today we live in a world where there is more choice than ever. But as wonderful as this is, it can also be overwhelming. As well as multiple career and family options, you have to choose where to live, whether to travel or do a master's degree, be a stay-at-home mum, work part-time, set up a business from home or, well, I could go on for ever ... And while having lots of options is exciting, it can also become crippling, and faced with so many big life decisions you can end up so fearful of making the wrong one that you avoid making any at all. With more choice comes more stress, and if you don't handle your choices correctly you can end up stuck in a rut, never breaking free of the comfort zone of home.

When you're confronted with so much choice, the best thing you can do is to home in on your core priorities. If you're debating what to have for lunch, but your priority is to eat quickly, then you can rule out a three-course meal and opt for a sandwich. If you're worried that all your friends are getting married and wonder if you should be doing the same, instead of signing up with every dating site you can find, ask yourself: is this really right for me?

Having said all this, the great thing about modern life is that although there may be too much choice, there's also plenty of flexibility. Most of us have had more than one relationship and at least two or three jobs – so it's OK to get it wrong. All you need is to know yourself well and prioritise what matters to you. Yes, there are lots of choices, but even if those you make do go pear-shaped, you can always go back to your parents or stay with friends or retrain. Just don't be afraid; if things don't work out, there's always a plan B.

The secret is adaptability: the happiest people are those who recognise that the world doesn't necessarily have a script for them and who roll with the punches. It's good to have ambition and goals, but don't be fooled by the *X Factor* idea that if you want something enough it will happen. Getting from A to B isn't always going to be a straight line and although if you try hard enough, you may get there, it may not be in the time frame you wanted. As you learn more about yourself, your partner or your job you're allowed to change your mind – don't become too fixated on 'success'. Because at different points in your life success will mean different things: it may be travelling or setting up a business or being able to spend weekends with your children. Just be prepared to adapt to any changes and you will succeed.

Relationships

When you do decide the time is right to go it alone and move out of home, you can suddenly become more aware that you're single and start to be concerned about it. Having a relationship today, sadly, has become another box for us to tick: we feel it is something that others are judging us by and worry that there's something wrong with us if we've not found that perfect person yet. This is made worse by social media sites such as Facebook that focus on our relationship status. Plus, we're constantly bombarded with questions from curious people asking about our love lives. 'Have you got a boyfriend? Oh, have you just broken up? Why aren't you seeing anyone? Are you a lesbian?'

In society's eyes it seems that having a partner makes life OK and represents success, whereas being single is something to worry about. An early episode of *Sex and the City* – 'They shoot single people, don't they?' – addresses the assumption that being single means you have more free time to spend with your friends. But Carrie Bradshaw soon finds out that your friends are always trying to set you up, arranging blind dates with what seem to be the dregs of society. Carrie points out that 'being alone has become the modern-day equivalent of being a leper' and feels that society stigmatises single people. The media feeds into this too by continuously focusing on the ups and downs of celebrities' love lives, struggling, for example, to understand that Cheryl Cole may be happy single, rather than pining for her ex or desperate to find a new man.

The theory seems to be that relationships are a meritocracy, whereby people who are in one deserve to be, while single, separated or divorced people do not, either because they are not good enough or because there is something wrong with them – somehow, it is their fault. Sure, having a relationship makes you feel valued and gives you status, but plenty of smart, beautiful young women are unattached. You should never put yourself down because you are 'still' single or feel rejected for not being with someone.

'All my friends are in relationships and slowly starting to tie the knot while I'm tired of the countless blind dates, one-night stands and being a third wheeler. I love being free and only having to think about myself, but Sundays and Valentine's

*Day really brought it home how lonely it can get. I
decided to give an old date another go ... I tried
stringing it along over a period of a few months,
convincing myself that it was working. I quickly
came to my senses and realised that there is no
emergency in settling down and not to feel
ashamed of being on my own.'*

Sarah, aged twenty-seven

If another area of your life is difficult, such as your job, or
you've fallen out with a close friend, the fact you're single
can make matters worse and can play to your fears that
you'll never find the right man. As time goes on, and you
become more aware of the ticking of your biological clock,
as well as your loneliness, the list of what I like to call your
non-negotiables may change drastically. You may start out
wanting a guy with a dry sense of humour, ambition, a love
of travel and no exes or baggage to deal with. But with the
passage of time, you may find yourself sacrificing what you
initially wanted until all that's left on your list is that you'd
like to meet a man, full stop. Don't be tempted to lower your
standards and date someone out of anuptaphobia, otherwise
known as the fear of being single (or of being married to the
wrong person).

Our idea of what we want from a boyfriend (or think we
want) can become distorted by Hollywood depictions of
relationships. So we might seek the 'perfect man' like
Edward Cullen (Robert Pattinson's character) in the *Twilight*
films or, conversely, someone who in normal circumstances

we would never go for but who, quite simply, has a penis and Y chromosome, as happens in the film *Knocked Up*. And the reality is that many women do settle; they believe they don't deserve any better, and therefore they accept less than they deserve.

Despite what you're fed by society, friends and the media, you need to remember that marriage and relationships aren't items on a checklist; entering into a serious relationship is a decision that should reflect how well you know yourself, what you want out of life, your hopes and beliefs and perhaps, most importantly, it should be something that enhances your life.

It's time we all accepted that there's nothing bad about being single. After all, there are currently 15.3 million women living alone in the UK – twice the number there were in 1970. And according to the US Census Bureau single women represent the fastest-growing part of the American population, with 42 per cent of women over eighteen having never been married. In a 2011 article entitled 'I'm a Loser, I'm Not Married, Let's Just All Look at Me: Ever-single Women's Perceptions of Their Social Environment' the authors Elizabeth Sharp and Lawrence Ganong looked at a small group of single women and the dilemmas facing them.[4] The piece identified that certain events acted as triggers in making the women feel bad. These included weddings, the throwing of the bouquet at weddings, a friend having a baby, Christmas Day and Valentine's Day. In addition, the group said they were made more aware of their single status when they were asked intrusive questions about their love lives and when people tried to set them up. They also said there were times when they felt 'invisible' and gave the example of being around their family when a younger sibling was married with children.

There are, of course, other studies showing that being single has no effect on how happy you are. An ongoing German study, for example, asks 30,000 people every year after the age of sixteen to rate their happiness from zero to ten.[5] What the study shows every time is that people who are married are happier around the wedding and honeymoon period, but after a time they revert back to being as happy – or as unhappy – as they were before marriage. In support of this idea is a survey in which women were asked how happy they were in their relationships: a significant number of them were in long-term relationships with or married to men they didn't see as their true love, but they stayed with them because it was comfortable or because they felt they had to for the sake of image.[6]

So the pressure to be chosen as someone's other half is often so intense that a lot of people would prefer to stay in an unhappy relationship than go it alone, but that should not be the case. Women – and men – should have enough of a sense of entitlement and self-esteem to choose a partner who makes their life easier, happier and more enjoyable, and not someone who is simply an alternative to being alone.

Getting on the Career Ladder

When you begin your first job it can be overwhelming. You may not know how to behave in the workplace – what is considered smart–casual office wear, for example? Do you need to ask when to take your lunch break? Can you joke with your boss?

It's really important to establish boundaries early on, as these will give you a clear idea about what is expected from you as a professional, as well as what you have the right to expect from your employers. Make a point of really getting to know your job description and the ethos of your company, in terms of both written and unwritten rules. For example, it may be stated clearly that your working day ends at 5pm, but if on the odd occasion you are asked to stay later for an important meeting and everyone else seems happy to pitch up, it's probably good to be aware of this sort of expectation. Likewise, when it comes to office relationships, different companies have different rules, so before you accept that dinner invitation from Jake in accounts make sure you know where you stand.

It's also vital to remember that the relationships you form at work are very different to the friendships you built at school and university. It can be difficult to work out whether the people you work with are your friends or just your colleagues and it's also hard to ensure boundaries in the workplace are enforced. Technology can often complicate things because it allows you to connect your social and private life with the people you work with who don't know much about you – so the posts, pictures and comments your friends find funny may not amuse your colleagues, for example. The authors of a 2008 study discuss how Facebook fosters what he refers to as 'ambient awareness', meaning that it encourages and supports weak relationships.[7] So through social media you may share in someone's private life despite them only sitting on reception where you work and having little to do with you or your work.

Being friends with your whole office on sites like Instagram or Facebook can also blur the lines between your social and professional, and people are likely to judge you based upon the information uploaded about you, rather than who you really are. So if you're snapped drunkenly kissing a guy in a club on a work night and your friends post it with comments about your hangover or how tipsy you were, colleagues may judge you as a wild party girl who doesn't take her career seriously, despite that night being a one-off.

On the other hand, online technology can help you to build a rapport with colleagues and can also be a good networking tool, helping you work your way up in your career through links and videos about your industry or job.[8] So social networking at work can be an asset or a liability, depending on how you choose to use it.

Disconnected

It is ironic that in an age where technology makes connecting so much easier many argue that social media is contributing to a growing fear of feeling disconnected and lonely: we're more connected to people online than our grandparents could ever have imagined, yet we are all still so scared of being alone.[9] OK, so you may have 650 Facebook friends, 1000 Twitter followers and more on Instagram, but social media can be really isolating. This is because we are not connecting with others in a real way when we 'chat' online – there is no physical contact and a computer or phone screen allows us to monitor our reactions more, so that we tend not to go with our gut feelings. As American writer Jonathan Safran Foer said in the *New York Times*: 'Technology celebrates connectedness, but encourages retreat ... each step forward has made it easier, just a little, to avoid the emotional work of being present by conveying information rather than humanity.'[10] So thanks to technology – predominantly mobiles, tablets, computers and the internet – we are so removed from the physical world of meeting people face to face that we're now obsessed instead with our relationships in the online world.

'I have to work weekends and the only way I can catch up with my friends is online or through WhatsApp. It's great for when we can't meet up for dinner or drinks, but sometimes I'd just love a hug from my best friend and I feel like we've drifted a bit because all we do is talk online now and rarely meet up.'

Hannah, aged twenty-four

Spending time online helps you to connect and share with the people in your life; however, loneliness can be fuelled considerably by a lack of real-life sociability. And we also tend to look on our Facebook news feed more when we're bored and lonely, which only fuels those emotions even more. How many of you recognise this scenario, for example: you are having a Saturday night in with a takeaway and you check your Facebook news feed to see what everyone else is up to. An ex-colleague has tagged herself at a cool restaurant, your best friend has bought a designer bag and your housemates have shared photos of a night out partying – all while you're at home, alone. So instead of feeling entertained by what you see on Facebook, you start to feel upset – in fact, you feel boring, alone and discontent with your life.

The way we are conducting relationships in the twenty-first century through text messages and online is altering our interactions. We find it easier to express ourselves behind the mask of a computer or phone screen as it feels less daunting than talking in person. And while this can make us feel more confident about starting up a conversation, which can work in our favour sometimes, it may also backfire. This is exactly what happens to Jesse Eisenberg, as Facebook creator Mark Zuckerberg in the film *The Social Network*: he sends a friend request to his ex-girlfriend, waits a few moments before clicking to see when she last was online and whether the request has been read, then starts to wonder why she hasn't responded, imagining the worst. Something a fair few of us are guilty of too . . .

'I'd been with my ex just over three years when he broke up with me over the phone. When I checked Facebook I was completely devastated to see he'd changed his status to single and all the girls that I *knew fancied him had 'liked' it. Facebook made it harder to get over him as I constantly saw what he was getting up to, and who he was with. I struggled to accept that he'd moved on so quickly, especially when I saw photos of him and a new girl smiling on a day out together.'*

Casey, aged twenty-eight

Me-ism

A lot of theorists suggest that today's celebrity culture, materialism, the fall of big political institutions and new technology have set up an atmosphere that is more conducive to a self-focused society. All attention is on 'the self' – how *we* look, how *we* feel, what *we* want – and with this comes the danger of distancing ourselves from friends and other people. Over time we have inflated our own egos, so that we now have a false sense of self-worth; friendships have suffered as a result and we have all become alone together.

The internet and electronic communications have the potential to feed feelings of disconnectedness, potentially making people start to pull away from the urban family ideal; we are no longer as close to each other, and the dream of having housemates and close pals – like in the sitcom *Friends* – has become harder to realise. Most of us struggle to have empathy for our friends and it's destroying our relationships.

Social networking can create pressure to constantly keep up to date with everything that is going on around us – to attend the opening of the hottest bar in town, wear the latest trends and live in the best area – when we could just be happy watching TV at home in our PJs. Reality TV shows such as *Made in Chelsea* and *The Only Way Is Essex* don't help matters either; while they can be great fun to watch, they do tend to make us obsess over postcodes, making us believe that where we live determines how successful we are and our pecking order in society.

With celebrities' faces and opinions constantly popping up on Twitter, on the cover of magazines and on TV it's impossible to escape their influence. We want to have their bodies, wardrobes, cars and homes because we want to relate to the same success and money that they have, even if it means we can only afford a Chanel phone case, rather than the entire collection. We live in a world of materialism, despite many of us having less than healthy finances, and it can be extremely difficult to deal with not having enough money to go out and party or see friends.

This can also affect individual friendships as well as friendship groups: if your group of friends are all going away for their birthdays and it's costing you £300 every time, it can cause tension as the pressure to 'have it all' starts to consume your life. You may have set yourself high expectations when going it alone, but it's OK to accept that you won't always be able to meet these.

The American TV series *Girls* is a perfect example of what life in the twenty-first century can be like for young women. Fans of the show will have seen how Hannah, Marnie, Jessa and Shoshanna – four twenty-somethings – come up against some of the worst parts of modern life, from unpaid internships to needy boyfriends, bad relationships and terrible sex. Other than being great entertainment, it is also a brilliant reflection of modern life and the struggle that so many girls in their twenties are facing in order to be financially independent, have a great career and be sexually satisfied.

So Now What?

This all sounds depressing for a girl in her twenties, right? But it doesn't have to be. You just have to learn to adapt.

A vital stage of breaking out on your own is accepting you can't have it all – and, more importantly, asking yourself why on earth you really *want* it all. What will having it all achieve? Is it really sustainable or have we all just bought into one idea of success and happiness, in the same way that we have all bought into one notion of beauty? We are conditioned to believe that other people will be more aware of us if we have a certain set of things – a particular job, specific labels in our wardrobe, a cool house in an expensive area – but we have to have these things for the right reasons.

Get back to basics and do what you say you want to do: if you want to be a writer, start a blog; if you want to be a CEO and set up a Fortune 500 company, do an MBA.

Of course, dreams don't always come true and disappointment is a huge part of life. You may lose your job, for example, and life might not be the way you imagined, but it's how you adapt to the changes and letdowns that determines your success. We're all prone to Disneyfying life sometimes, but we have to be adaptable. We may suffer metaphorical blows, but we have to be tolerant to these and get back up again.

When faced with too many decisions, ask yourself what you are really achieving by keeping as many options open as possible. Try to focus on just one or two things that you are willing to work on and remember that even your dream job is going to be horrible at times. Be the best you can be and be willing to progress and change.

Going it alone can also make you alarmingly aware of things like being single. We live in a society that tells us if you're good enough you'll find the right guy and you'll get married. But that's simply not true. We all know people whose personalities leave a lot to be desired, but who are in relationships, and we all know some really wonderful people who just happen to be single. We are social beings and we function well when we have the right person to give us support, but the operative word here is *right*. We're poisoned with all this 'you-complete-me' rubbish – you should already feel complete as a person before you enter into any sort of relationship. Searching for someone to give you a sense of wholeness is a recipe for disaster.

It's not meant to be easy going it alone for the first time. It's supposed to be exciting, but also scary and it does, inevitably, make you think and wonder if you're doing the right thing. The only way to grow and gain confidence as an individual is by doing something that you never thought you could do; if all you did was stay in your comfort zone, you wouldn't evolve emotionally. So, as daunting as these 'firsts' may seem, embrace them with the confidence that: a) you are not on your own – everyone is to some extent facing similar challenges; b) although you do need human contact, you don't need hundreds of friends, just two or three genuine mates to get you through life; and c) it's all a learning curve, so whether it's a relationship or a job, don't be afraid to make mistakes because they are, ultimately, one of the few things that we do in life that give us a real sense of what we do and don't want.

CHAPTER 8

•

Quarter-life Crisis and the Fear of Getting Older

'I always feel like I could be doing more,
or that I should be doing better; I look around
and it seems I'm losing the race to wherever it is
I'm supposed to be, and that somehow I'm
always falling short. It sounds crazy, but
sometimes I feel old already.'

Sienna, aged twenty-three

The other day I was looking through a magazine and noticed an ad for a wrinkle cream that claimed to stop the signs of ageing and keep you looking young and beautiful – the model in the ad, incidentally, looked about twenty. A few pages later there was a feature on 'school days' parties, showing grown women dressed up in schoolgirl outfits, complete with knee-high socks, tiny pleated skirts and ponytails. And then, a few pages after that, tween models – probably about nine or ten years old – were depicted walking and laughing together in another ad, styled and dressed to look much older, like a Gap version of a *Sex and the City* promo.

And that's when it hit me: we live in a world where social equity for women seems to peak when we are ridiculously young. Models look like teenage girls (even those advertising anti-ageing products), adult women spend billions every year on cosmetics and surgery trying to look like teenage girls and, thanks to the wonderful world of online porn, it seems that most men would rather have sex with 'barely legal' teenage girls (except for those who have a fetish for MILFs or 'naughty grandmas' which, in porn-land, refers to women as young as those in their thirties or forties – charming). To complicate things further, due to the visual nature of social networking and how we engage online (as discussed in Chapter 5), we fall victim to the pressures previously faced only by Hollywood starlets, whose fear of becoming irrelevant in a world so dominated by youth and beauty is well documented.

Forever Young

It seems that increasingly the world is manufactured for the enjoyment of youth. You might believe that youth has always been highly regarded, but this is a relatively new trend. In fact, back in the early 1900s the concept of teenagers did not even exist. There were no culture norms to unite them or institutions that developed peer-group attachment on a large scale. Fast-forward a century and teen culture today is omnipresent – not only are there more teenagers, but there is also more of an emphasis on youth and youth culture now than ever before. Teenagers have become highly sought-after consumers, trendsetters, icons of fashion and music, and even online celebs.

But how did we get here? Well, the single most important factor in creating teenage culture was the dramatic rise in secondary-school attendance. Between 1910 and 1930 enrolment in secondary schools increased almost 400 per cent. And, as enrolment grew, the student body changed. So whereas before that time only the privileged elite could go to secondary school, all of a sudden students came from all socioeconomic, ethnic and racial backgrounds and what united them most – the defining factor they all had in common – was their youth.

Around the 1950s, this brand-new exciting social group caught the attention of marketeers. They saw the potential of treating teens as consumers with purchasing power and style preferences. The idea was that selling products to younger people meant that they would be better consumers for longer. The idea worked. In fact, it worked so well that eventually the TV companies, record studios and movie industry followed suit and started marketing directly to appeal to 'the youth'. And so youth culture began to be celebrated by society in a way that it had never before been in human history. Of course, youth and beauty were valued by the ancient Greeks and Romans, but so were wisdom and experience – something that is increasingly being ignored in the age-phobic, youth-obsessed culture we live in today. And although we have always admired bright, young things, our preoccupation with the connotations of youth (beauty, naivety, impulsivity) seems fundamentally different now from ever before. In a recent large-scale report, 63 per cent of those surveyed felt that society's obsession with youth has got out of hand.[1]

It's no real surprise, therefore, that this obsession with youth, anxiety about life passing you by and the quarter-life crisis have become big issues. In fact, according to a survey conducted by the American Psychological Association, Millennials (people born after 1980) are the most stressed-out generation of all. While older age groups reported that their stress was on the decline, Millennials reported an average stress level of 5.4 out of 10 – and just to be clear, on this particular scale anything over 3.6 is considered unhealthy. The survey's authors report that not only are younger Americans experiencing the most stress, they say they are not managing it well either.[2]

Sorry, the Lifestyle You Ordered Is Out of Stock

'I think the hardest thing is that it feels like life should have been better – should have been more sorted by now. I look around and everyone else seems to have it more figured out than I do ... It's a weird feeling – being young, theoretically, but still feeling like you're running out of time.'

Meghan, aged twenty-eight

So why all the stress and quarter-life angst? It seems that what may be underlying this is the fear of somehow either missing out on or misusing youth. A deep concern about overlooking something better manifests in everything from constantly checking phones for messages to having trouble making even simple choices for fear that making the wrong one will mean missing out in some way.

Part of this lies in the way that youth is portrayed today – because while the aesthetic aspects are not new, there is something else going on: there seems to be a bigger onus on success and achievement. Lists like the 'Forbes 30 under 30' and media sources like Young Hollywood seem to be everywhere and, even if you try and ignore them, they somehow sneak into your consciousness by a kind of media osmosis, eliciting, in equal measure, admiration, envy and panic.

We often hear about and discuss how idealised images of beauty are distorting the way we see ourselves, but equally, the idealised portrayals of success and achievement also serve as a backdrop to how we assess our lives. And boy do we assess them. We now have hi-tech versions of the old-fashioned 'clap-o-meters' giving us feedback on every decision, thought and musing. The number of 'likes', 'friends', 'pokes' and 'followers' we have gives us an insight into how well we're doing or, perhaps more significantly, how we are doing in relation to others. And this is, again, where things are different now. A couple of decades ago a story or two might have circulated about how old classmates were faring, and someone might have felt slightly perturbed that the guy with questionable personal hygiene they'd turned down for the school dance had become a millionaire. But today anyone's life can be – and is – there online for all to see. And the irony is that what you're reacting to is probably not even the reality of your peers' successes, but an embellished version of their lives. Also, the people most likely to post information about their careers are those who are doing well anyway, while those who may (like most) be struggling keep schtum about their difficulties, so that it seems as though absolutely everyone is doing better than you.

Feelings of unease or envy when confronted with the success stories of peers are not a new phenomenon; however, there are some aspects that are different today. Although in previous generations most people hadn't made *The Times* Rich List by their thirties, they were able to feel independent by leaving their parents' homes, buying their own places and getting into jobs that seemed to offer at least some semblance of career progression: all things that indicated a successful start to adult life, both to themselves and those around them. Today, however, the focus is not just on success but on being successful as quickly as possible. The mantra seems to be 'younger = better' and this affects everything from our body image to the expectations that we have about our romances to how satisfied we feel in our careers.

One of the things that I hear when I speak to my Millennial colleagues and friends is that they have a sense of not living fast enough or achieving enough before ... well, I'm never clear what the deadline is, but it seems to have something to do with a statute of limitations on when accomplishment ceases to be cool – winning an Oscar in your twenties, making your first million before you're thirty . . . Maybe it's because we live in such a visual society that we can only imagine ourselves being able to enjoy success when we are young and beautiful.

Part of this, no doubt, also comes from the fact that the majority of careers in the spotlight begin early. But again, this is also because of the nature of the industries we hear about the most. Be it Hollywood or music or online entrepreneurship, success in these fields seems to go hand in hand with youth, so by the time you're in your late twenties there is the sense of having missed the boat. Yet, ironically, while on the one hand we revere young Hollywood for being so successful so fast, we are never really surprised at the burnout and emotional meltdown that ensue for many of them, probably precisely because they got successful too young.

We also need to acknowledge that all this is playing out behind a curtain of uncertainty when it comes to the current job market. The fast-paced changes due to technology mean that many jobs are being made obsolete – or, as Barack Obama said: the jobs of the future don't even exist today. I'm guessing that hearing this, rather than filling you with hope and awe about where you are headed might, instead, imbue you with a genuine and well-founded sense of concern that what you learning or the skills you are investing in won't be needed for much longer – not to mention, as trend forecaster Maude Standish notes in her blog: 'Many Millennials are hired because of their youth, which is diminishing as you read this . . .'[3]

From Here to Reality

In Chapter 1 we looked at the therapeutic model known as Person Centred Therapy, which explains how happy or well-adjusted we feel by looking at the difference between our real selves and our ideal selves; to put it simply, how content we feel with life depends on how much the reality of who we are meets our expectations of who we should be.

Now it turns out that this can be a real issue for a generation raised on the idea that they are really special. I think what happened can, at least to some extent, be traced back to the 1970s when discussion of the whole concept of entitlement and self-esteem began in the media in relation to child-rearing. In order to improve their kids' chances of success in school and later in life, parents tried to instil a really good sense of self-esteem. They did this by telling little girls that they were perfect princesses and little boys that they were super cool like rock stars; by ensuring that everyone got a participation medal at school sports days – no losers, just lots of winners who had all done amazingly well just by being there; by telling all children their drawings were masterpieces, no matter how (inadvertently) Pollockesque they were, etc. It should be noted that the intention was well placed (even if the execution was less so), but we have since learned that when you try and boost self-esteem in the wrong way (i.e. by saying *everything* your kid does is fab), there is a real danger that you'll boost narcissism instead.

In her 2009 book which looks at narcissism, Jean Twenge explains that using the platitudes and superlatives proclaiming the specialness of our offspring actually leads to disappointment when this view is not confirmed by the rest of the world.[4] In a great piece in *Time* magazine in 2013, Joel Stein noted that: 'This generation has the highest likelihood of having unmet expectations with respect to their careers and the lowest levels of satisfaction with their careers at the stage they are at. It's a crisis of unmet expectations.' And here are some of the thought-provoking stats quoted in the article:

- 40 per cent of Millennials think they should be promoted every two years – regardless of performance.
- Three times as many middle-school girls want to grow up to be a PA to a famous person as want to be a senator, according to a 2007 study.
- Four times as many girls would pick a celeb PA job over being the CEO of a major corporation
- The incidence of narcissistic personality disorder is nearly three times as high for people in their twenties as for the generation that's now sixty-five and older, according to the National Institutes of Health.[5]

Given that the perfect storm – of politics, economics and social child-rearing trends – has come together to ensure that, for most young people, their real and their ideal selves are as disparate as they can be, it's no surprise that the sense of not being where (or even who) you're supposed to be is becoming increasingly common.

A Job for Life?

When it comes to careers, it seems that there has been a shift from the baby-boomers' 'Keep-calm-and-carry-on' mantra that focused on economic security and pragmatism and, indeed, even from the mindset of those who started their careers in the eighties and nineties, when the economic prosperity of the time saw a positivity around career progression. Instead, today there seems to be a sense that careers need to be 'special' to be fulfilling.

While the general thinking in this area is that the problem is the sense of entitlement that has been engendered in today's Millennial generation, writer and professor Cal Newport – himself a Millennial – suggests that it may have more to do with the fact that there is an insidious side to the 'follow-your-passion' advice that has prevailed over the past couple of decades. According to his research, use of the phrase 'follow your passion' began its rise in the early 1990s, peaking around 2000 – precisely the time when many Millennials were in their formative school years.[6] Interestingly, in a great article on the site waitbutwhy.com the authors note that at the same time that this was happening, expressions like 'a fulfilling career' were on the rise too, whereas 'a secure career' went out of style,[7] indicating a real shift in what we began to expect to get out of our professional lives and, indeed, what we expected to put into them.

So while today there is still, of course, a need for financial independence and making lots of money, there seems to be the added dimension of needing to find our *career soulmate* –

a job that 'completes' us. And whereas previous generations seemed to be clear about the fact that hard work and time were needed to get to a place where things began to feel rewarding, and that at times it might be, well, not so fulfilling, the 'talent show' society we live in today makes it seem like all you really need to succeed is a) to want it enough and b) to be special enough. But if we're entering jobs thinking that passion trumps hard work, it's no surprise that job satisfaction isn't there. And, just for the record, most uber-successful people who have noteworthy careers were *so* not there in their twenties.

Loving your job is great – and it's true that you are more likely to succeed if you actually like what you do. But the thing is, no matter how well suited you are to your career, there will be times when it doesn't feel easy. There will be times when you are tired and uncertain and when the fulfilment is not there to the extent that you'd hoped. Also, really importantly, it's not so much the passion that you have for a job before you do it that matters, but rather, it's the passion that you develop for it gradually, which comes from hard work and overcoming obstacles and even getting it wrong sometimes. From his research in the area, Newport notes that successful people don't necessarily 'follow their passion' – rather, they build on their core interests, develop a solid skill set and then use those skills to build a career.[8] So while the 'follow-your-passion'-style career guidance suggests all you need to do is figure out what you really love and then match it to a job, the problem is this: in most cases passion is not enough; in fact, according to research, the quest for passion can actually corrode job satisfaction.[9] So the big take-home message here, which I have to agree with, is this: rather than thinking in terms of 'find your passion and you'll do great work', there is something to be said for 'do great work and you'll find your passion'.

I love my job – I genuinely do – but the truth is that I loved it more the better I got at it and the more I saw that I was making a difference. In a way, it became less about me feeling good and more about doing something that mattered, making an impact; and I don't mean this to sound worthy or sentimental – it's just that the platitudes (about wanting it enough being enough) are not true and they can, in fact, be dangerous if you buy into the idea that that is all it takes.

In one of the coolest commencement speeches I've heard (no, not Steve Jobs'), comedian Tim Minchin talked at the University of Western Australia about how – contrary to common belief – you don't have to have a great big dream to strive for, but rather, you should focus on the passionate pursuit of short-term goals. He makes the point that being 'micro-ambitious' – i.e. putting your head down and working as hard as you can on whatever is in front of you – is key, explaining that by focusing too much on your dream, you risk becoming too rigid and losing sight of other opportunities or 'the shiny thing out of the corner of your eye'. I love this idea: the notion that long-term goals are fine, but that making the most of and doing the best at whatever you are working on now can lead to alternative long-term goals you never imagined. Success, therefore, isn't about a particular destination, job or salary package, but the meaningful dedication to what you are doing right now. And this has been my experience. So if I can give you any advice as a psychologist, or even just as someone lucky enough to love their job most of the time: work hard, even on days when it's tough, and don't be afraid to change your mind as you learn about yourself and your field; stand up, take risks and see mistakes and disappointments as absolutely inevitable, but never as defining.

We're used to instant gratification, but one of the things that psychologists have known for years is that delaying gratification, learning how to put in the work and wait for the reward, is key to success in later life.

The Stanford marshmallow experiments, a famous series of studies on delayed gratification, were conducted in the early 1960s and 1970s by Stanford University psychologist Walter Mischel. In the experiment, individual children were offered a treat, like a marshmallow or cookie. They were left in a room with the treat and given the choice to eat it immediately or to wait about fifteen minutes until the experimenter returned, when they would be rewarded with two treats. Most of the children couldn't cope with waiting, but around a third of them managed it. The researchers then followed up to see how the same kids were doing years later, and looked at differences between those who were able to defer gratification and those who gave in to temptation. And here is the interesting thing: they found that the children who were able to wait were described by those around them as significantly more competent. In fact, they were shown to have better outcomes in life on several different measures, including academic aptitude,[10] educational attainment[11] and even body mass index.[12]

In life, sometimes the results we expect from our efforts don't happen as quickly as we want them to – and while we live in a world that increasingly glamourises and focuses on the simplicity and speed of success as a means to inspire us, it's important that we don't feel let down when success doesn't come as easily as we expected it would. So when searching for work or embarking on your dream career, remember that the expectation of instant gratification is not realistic. Take the time to explore your strengths, pursue a career that *you* can grow in, learn from and be good at, rather than one that you think meets the expectations of others and don't be afraid to get it wrong. You may be experiencing a quarter-life crisis, but the fact is you are young enough to get it wrong, change your mind and learn from your mistakes; it is precisely these mistakes that will give you the grit and perspective to do well in the future.

Mirror Mirror

So we've established that the predominant message in a youth-obsessed culture is that youth equals happiness. And if this is the case, then looking young is going to be high up there in terms of your priorities.

Now the search for the fountain of youth has been around for ever, but today our preoccupation with age reversal seems to have become inextricably linked with our sense of self-worth. And since things have become so youth-centric we now have this weird situation whereby kids are feeling the pressure to look older and adults feel pressure to look younger in an attempt to conform to idealised notions of youth and beauty.

The message *look young* (as is the case with the message *look thin*) is now like background noise – so pervasive that you never notice it yet, paradoxically, you always know it's there. So 'You look young' is a compliment, of course, laden with connotations about attractiveness, desirability, health and beauty, while critiquing clothes or hairstyles as looking 'too grown up' or 'mature' is an insult; we talk about getting makeovers that will 'take years off' or about getting cosmetic surgery (currently being promoted as a 'lifestyle lift') to make us feel *happier* about who we are. And these anti-ageing messages are no longer confined to the glossy magazines and makeover shows; they are online and advertised on sites where young people – even teens who really shouldn't even be remotely concerned about ageing – are spending most of their time. The effects of this are evident in the number of young people deciding to undergo cosmetic procedures, the steepest increase (including so-called 'preventative Botox') being among young women and girls in their teens and twenties.

A 2014 survey by teen website WOWGO found that two-thirds of girls in the UK aged twelve to fourteen wanted cosmetic surgery (mostly the removal of fat from their stomachs and hips or breast implants), while according to a report by the American Society of Plastic Surgeons, there was a 100 per cent increase in the injection of Botox and Dysport into Americans aged thirteen to nineteen (predominantly girls) from the late 1990s to 2013, and a whopping 509 per cent increase across all ages over the same period.[13] Indeed, as Vivian Diller, a New York-based psychologist dealing with body-image issues, notes in a 2013 article, around a quarter of a million teens in 2010 in the US had cosmetic surgery to improve their appearance.[14] The demedicalisation of these procedures, coupled with the fact that they are so accessible and cheap, means that they no longer serve solely as a route to looking younger but, worryingly, as a quick fix to poor self-esteem.

The fact that celebrity worship has become such an integral part of our culture also seems to underscore the quest for youth. The notion that to be relevant means staying young and thin is perpetuated by the entertainment industry, where women are portrayed either as heroines for taking on Mother Nature and defying the sands of time or as tragic figures, forgotten and ignored because they had the audacity to age.

Perhaps getting older is so scary because, in effect, we airbrush older people out of popular culture. While it is estimated that one in three people in the West is now aged fifty or over, this is certainly not reflected in what we see on that social barometer of what's acceptable – the media. High-profile cases of TV presenters – like fifty-five-year-old Miriam O'Reilly, who successfully sued the BBC for age discrimination after being fired form *Countryfile* in 2009, or Selina Scott, who won a payout and an apology from Channel Five following her replacement with a younger presenter in 2008 when she was fifty-seven – underscore the idea that the media isn't sure where women who aren't young should fit. And sadly, I think that is true for a lot of women as well. If we buy into the idea that our value lies in our youth and beauty, then no wonder the passage of time can be felt be so desperately and intensely. We need to develop self-esteem that is reliant on something less transient than perfect skin and perky breasts! Yes, looking young and pretty is great, but there are a lot of other great things about you that aren't as susceptible to the passage of time: your passions, your beliefs and talents, the things and people you love, your creativity, your wisdom – all the things that make you you.

Getting older in today's society is hard – even if you are still young. The truth is, however, that we are constantly changing, and growth is a normal part of our development, whatever age we are at. Being scared of that change means that we pointlessly try and cling on to a version of ourselves that is no longer relevant to who we are. Getting older, as is the case with anything to do with body image in my opinion, comes down to a sense of entitlement – guys age better simply because they feel they are *allowed* to; they are entitled to have grey hair and expression lines and even lose the six-pack. And while some will say, 'Well that's just evolution', I don't think it's as simple as that.

Firstly, we are taught to value youth and beauty in women above all other attributes, whereas for men it's success and money (both unaffected by age) that count; secondly, we are led to fear age. We need to reassess what we celebrate women for, what we fall back on to boost our self-esteem and, perhaps most importantly, each and every one of us needs to remember that the essence of who we are should not be reduced to a bunch of physical features that will inevitably change in time. Know what you value about yourself, and don't allow an image-obsessed culture to make you feel 'less than' – no one and nothing can do that unless you give them permission to do so.

Conflict, Confusion and Crisis

> When I was young, there were very few elders willing to talk about their darkness; most of them pretended that success was all they had ever known ... I thought I had developed a unique and terminal case of failure. I did not realise I had merely embarked on a journey towards joining the human race.
>
> Parker Palmer, author, educator and activist[15]

Taking stock of life, of how we are doing and of how far we have come, isn't something that only happens on New Year's Eve or birthdays. It's something that occurs throughout life, especially after major changes. The renowned developmental psychologist Erik Erikson proposed the notion that we undergo a life crisis soon after we leave the safety and familiarity of home and enter the 'real world'.[16] But given the changes that the real word has seen over the past few decades, the basics of intimacy versus isolation that Erikson put forward don't quite capture the whole picture.

Your twenties are supposed to be an exciting, productive and relatively carefree time before the stress of mortgages and childcare take hold. However, the UK charity the Depression Alliance estimates that a third of twenty-somethings feel depressed and, according to Dr Oliver Robinson and a team of researchers at the University of Greenwich and Birkbeck University, quarter-life crises are a very real phenomenon, occurring typically between the ages of twenty-five and thirty-five. Like the mid-life crisis, they involve a sense of disappointment, insecurity and loneliness and, interestingly, the researchers note that educated professionals are those most likely to suffer.[17]

The themes put forward by Robinson and his team include four phases, namely:

- feeling 'locked in' – to a job or relationship or both
- a growing sense that change is possible
- a period of rebuilding a new life
- the cementing of fresh commitments that reflect new interests, aspirations and values.

When the authors presented the findings of their study at a conference in 2013 they were quick to reassure that it's not all bad news. While the quarter-life crisis lasts an average of two years, it is very often a catalyst for positive change, and 80 per cent of those interviewed actually looked back on theirs in a positive way. Not only that, but experiencing a quarter-life crisis apparently reduces the risk of suffering a full-blown mid-life crisis later on.

As we've seen, being twenty today is different from even a generation ago. You are socialised into expecting more from your life and yourself than your parents did. You need to fight harder for a first job, work harder to save money for a first home and manage a social-media landscape that can make you feel never quite good enough.

A study from the University of Essex found that 86 per cent of the 1100 twenty-somethings questioned suffered from FOMO – a fear of missing out (see also page 71) and not doing enough with their lives.[18] The researchers then looked at a sample of more than 2000 adults aged between eighteen and sixty-five and found that those with the most intense feelings of FOMO were individuals who didn't feel engaged, nurtured and acknowledged in their lives.

A student of mine recently explained, 'You're supposed to be young and carefree and having fun, but all the time you're thinking: I'm not doing what I thought I would be at this point. You're constantly focused on what you haven't achieved yet, so can't really enjoy being young.'

It seems that FOMO, comparing oneself with everyone on Facebook and the youth-obsessed culture we live in have become the unholy trinity making the quarter-life crisis an increasingly common developmental milestone.

Performance Anxiety

Perhaps the fact that many people today are having babies and settling down at a later stage than previous generations, so putting off the big decisions, is making other decisions harder too. Is a general indecisiveness contributing to the quarter-life crisis that's affecting so many? There is a strong desire to do something amazing, yet those first steps on the path to wherever it is you feel you are destined to be look so difficult and so a sense of existential angst sets in.

Too much choice is notorious for making decisions hard. And given that there are so many scenarios floating around everywhere, detailing the choices you could/should/ought to be making, it may be the case that you end up feeling paralysed by indecision. What if you pick the wrong partner? End up with a good job, but not one that makes you feel as contented as you thought you'd be?

Given the fact that there is so much expectation of what needs to be achieved by the time you reach your twenties, experiencing a quarter-life crisis is, frankly, understandable. But you need to remember that while you may feel a great sense of performance anxiety, wanting to prove to the world that you can reach your goals in record time, it is vital that you learn to separate reality from unrealistic or impractical expectations. That doesn't mean that you shouldn't be ambitious – just that you should ensure your ambitions are yours and not born of a need to prove to others how well you can perform. A good place to start is by questioning cultural definitions of success and how much you agree with them. Think about what you want out of life, rather than trying to beat the clock; being happy feels good at any age, regardless of what the cultural messages you are bombarded with will tell you.

Self-care Skills

With the ever-growing pressure that characterises our times, it's easy to forget that doing well is not just about making money or career progression – it's actually about being physically and mentally healthy and stable. A happy life is about meaning and sustainability and they come not from working so hard that you burn out, but from ensuring that you invest in your own wellbeing as well as in your career. You do this by making small changes to how you value yourself, your time and those around you.

Pace yourself when it comes to the hours that you work; it may be tempting to work every weekend and always be the first person into the office every morning, but if you do this for too long, some other area of your life will suffer. Instead, ensure that you have time to de-stress with friends and that those really simple things you take for granted – like eating right and sleeping well – are, well, not taken for granted! Burnout is a real problem, affecting your ability not only to work effectively, but also the way you are able to draw out any pleasure or gain experience in any meaningful way. When you lose sight of what is realistic, you also lose sight of what is important, so make time to ask yourself the question: is there balance in my life?

Take time out in the day to focus on important relationships. Whether it's a five-minute call with your mum or sending an email to touch base with a friend you haven't been in contact with for a while, nurturing yourself through nurturing those important relationships around you is integral to wellbeing and balance. When it comes to technology, try to set boundaries that you can live with. I try not to look at emails after around 7.30pm, as that is my family time; it's the time I set aside for Jessie and Teddy – to eat and talk and just be there with them. Doing that gives me a clear sense of where work ends, and so winding down becomes easier.

Sleep is another important factor. It sounds simple, but make sure you get enough of it! There is an abundance of research out there on the importance of getting seven to eight hours a night, so work it in to your daily routine.

People often talk about exercise as something that needs to be done to get into shape for a big event or to fit into a favourite dress. The fact is, however, that the benefits of integrating exercise into your routine are amazing for both your physical and mental health. As such, finding a sport or activity that you like and making the time to do it consistently is really important for your overall sense of wellbeing.

Everyone talks about never having enough time to get everything done. So learn to prioritise and, more importantly, to acknowledge the reality that certain things will simply *not* get done. Being able to tolerate an incomplete to-do list is important.

Know that everyone, regardless of how 'well' they seem to be doing, questions where they're going with their life at some point. Having a prestigious career doesn't mean that you're exempt from existential angst – it just means that you probably have more money and less time to deal with it. Be reassured by the fact that you are not alone, and find people you can share your problems with in a way that won't make you feel judged. In this age of self-promotion and self-delusion it's so comforting to be able to have an honest discussion about your anxieties, fears and perceived shortcomings with someone who shares these feelings and can really empathise.

In short, learn to take care of *you*. Self-care skills are vital to your success and achievement. And being honest, working hard and having the integrity to stick to your ideals all contribute, too. Do whatever job you are doing to the best of your abilities. Doing a job well, keeping promises and following through are fundamental.

So Now What?

Stop looking to your left and right, trying to emulate the lives of those around you and focus instead on living yours. You may not be able to buy a house as quickly as your parents did or land a job or your dream guy the way that your best friend has, but that doesn't matter. Life is not a race and other people's successes or failures have no bearing on yours, so comparing is pointless and a waste of time. And, frankly, there are few decisions you'll make in your twenties that will make or break your entire life.

So let go of those soul-destroying beliefs of how amazing your life should have become by now before the irrational expectations on which these are based prevent you from reaching your goals and full potential. It would also help to make a more concerted effort to a) not put on a 'My-Life-is-Amazing' show and b) not get too obsessed with watching others' 'My-Life-is-Amazing' shows. You are not the only one feeling like this; it's just that you, like everyone else your age, have grown up learning the importance of building a personal brand and so sharing what's *really* going on isn't easy.

Author, educator and activist Parker Palmer has spoken

about how we often misunderstand not just the things that we are supposed to believe in, but faith itself. In a speech he gave in 1992 he addressed the issue of what we choose to believe in:

> Faith is not a set of beliefs we are supposed to sign up for. It is instead the courage to face our illusions and allow ourselves to be disillusioned by them. It is the courage to walk through our illusions and dispel them. Not everything is measurable and yet so much of what we do has that yardstick applied to it. Another illusion is 'I am what I do ... My worth comes from my functioning. If there is to be any love for us, we must succeed at something.' We are not what we do. We are who we are. The rigors of trying to be faithful involve being faithful to one's gifts, faithful to others' reality, faithful to the larger need in which we are all embedded, faithful to the possibilities inherent in our common life.[19]

I love this quote because it conceptualises faith as courage – the courage to persevere or to walk away from what isn't working – and I think this that is key when going through any crisis. Perhaps the answers that we want aren't immediately obvious, but there is always something to be said for focusing on resolution through questions rather than answers. The great thing about being the age you are now is that there is lots of time to learn and grow from poor decisions and mistakes and to change your mind.

If you are starting to feel stuck in an area of your life, be it a relationship or at work, then take action. And that doesn't mean bolting out of the door every time things don't feel right – it means confronting the issue. So tell your boyfriend why things aren't working, so that he has a chance to make things better. That way, you can be sure that before you walk away you have tried to make things work and it will, in turn, make it easier to stay away and have a clean break. Likewise, if you feel that your job isn't right, before you dramatically hand in your resignation and walk out Hollywood-movie style, think things through: ask for different responsibilities at your current workplace, put out feelers about others and figure out how your skill set can be used to help you move to where you want to be. Remember, you don't want to find yourself without a job and needing to cover rent at the end of the month. So make the big decisions, but make them strategically.

It may take a while to get over your quarter-life crisis, but actually, a lot of the soul-searching you're doing and the coping strategies for putting things into perspective – being true to what you want, not competing, carefully thinking through big moves and tweaking – will help you in the long term.

One of the things that I have done since my twenties that works for me – between all the worrying about what I still haven't achieved and which direction I ought to be going in – is to take just a few minutes every night to be grateful for what I have. Working hard for what you want and being grateful for what you have are not mutually exclusive. In fact, in my experience, focusing a little on what's right in your life is one of the best antidotes for getting too caught up in what may be wrong.

It's a normal part of development to experience a sense of uncertainty in your twenties. Transitions tend to start with endings – leaving home, breaking up with your partner, graduating from college – and each one will inevitably make you feel that you are leaving a bit of your old self behind and wondering who you ought to be now. But this stage isn't one you need to 'solve' or 'fix'; rather it is part of a process, an ongoing exploration of *you* – your passions, beliefs, desires, dislikes and . . . well, you get the picture: you need time to become the person you want to be.

Adulthood means finding your identity. As kids and teens, even in college, knowing who we are seems pretty straightforward: our grades, hobbies, the group we hang out with, our chosen degree – they all give us clear and easily defined ways to categorise ourselves. By the time we are into our twenties, things aren't so simple. But don't be afraid of that. In fact, enjoy the freedom to write your script, rather than having it thrust upon you. It's up to you what you buy into and what you reject. And while you might have to rewrite a few scenes or even rethink the plot, it's *your* life – so confront it, direct it and embrace it.

Conclusion

So, for all you twenty-somethings out there, what is the secret to navigating this decade successfully, when there is so much to do and figure out? Here's a quick recap of the key strategies:

Work

Pick a career that you like, not just one that fits in with your idea of the perfect career girl, but one that you will find it easier to pursue when you realise that there is no such thing.

Put yourself forward for projects; the people you work with will value the fact that you show up and pitch in, and even when it's not the most exciting thing in the world, having the integrity and professionalism to do your job as well as you can will make you good at it and people will notice. Also, really importantly, don't worry about not knowing what kind of career you want just yet – some of the most interesting people I've ever met had no idea what they wanted to be at twenty or even thirty and others were brave enough to change their minds even when they thought they did. Research has shown that twenty-somethings who do work are happier than those who don't or those who are underemployed, so even if you're not in the job of your dreams, it may be a step in the right direction. Learn as much as you can when you're on the first rungs of your career and don't worry if others around you seem to know more; it takes time to be really good at anything in life.

Looks

The idea that women are valued for their looks is nothing new, but the sheer number and the ubiquity of glamourised, perfected images around us make it seem as though a woman should be as close to physically perfect as humanly (or, perhaps more accurately, superhumanly) possible. But let's be clear here. Investing in your looks is fine – even a normal part of establishing your identity – but looking pretty is not a prerequisite for success and happiness or even for self-acceptance, and should never become yet another 'have-to' – another burden. The way you look does not define you, nor should you buy into the notion that you – or any of us – can reach the levels or physical perfection that you are encouraged to aspire to today.

Relationships

Firstly, relationships are not a meritocracy, so feeling there is something wrong with you until you're in one is, frankly, illogical. A relationship does not express your value as a human being, nor do commitment and marriage or settling down equate to lifelong romance, fireworks, mind-blowing sex and being 'complete'. Love and relationships should be about genuine human connection. So please don't worry if, all of a sudden, it seems like all your friends are pairing off while you are still manically flicking to the left on Tinder every Friday night. Don't torment yourself with questions like 'What's wrong with me? Why am I the one who's still single?' because the answer is simple: nothing is wrong; you are just single, so enjoy life, fill it with experiences and learning and discovery and connections – and you *will* meet someone you like because of who *they are*, not because you're looking for a relationship.

The media

Be media-savvy. By this I mean be critical about the ideas and products and beliefs that are being sold to you. We live in such a commercial, media-saturated world that it's hard to get away from the pop-culture marketplace and the implied value judgements about the way you should act, look and behave. But these messages are nothing more than marketeers' ideas of who you *should* be, and you can choose whether or not you buy into that. I'm not saying it's easy, but try to look at things with a more critical eye and, whether it's an ad for a beauty product using airbrushed models or a sexist music video or film that makes you

uncomfortable, get into the habit of questioning and challenging what you see around you.

Motherhood

I know this may not be on the radar yet for many of you,
but forewarned is forearmed: the blatant fetishisation of
pregnancy and motherhood over the last few years has distorted the beautiful miracle of giving birth, turning it into
an amalgam of unhealthy expectations regarding everything
from how and where we choose to give birth to how soon
we get back into our pre-pregnancy dress size. And it doesn't
stop there; we feel that our little bundles of joy need to be
the embodiment of the perfect lives we intend to manifest,
so we ensure that they are signed up to every toddler chess
class and mini-yoglatis group; then, if we are going back to
work, we justify our decision to all the other mums, explaining how this will definitely be better for baby. But hear this:
the point of parenting is not to create a superbaby or to
rebrand yourself as a supermum. It's about giggles and
smelly nappies, cuddles and competitive sleep deprivation
with your partner or friends. It's about exhilaration and
exhaustion and feeling conflicted and making mistakes and
even *not* fitting into your skinny jeans as quickly as you
thought you would. And that is OK because motherhood is
such an amazing human experience that holding it – or
yourself – up to an arbitrary and unrealistic set of rules and
beliefs detracts from the depth and the meaning of the
whole thing.

Home

Of all the things that should be getting easier in this day and age you would think that housework would be right up there, what with all the gadgets at our fingertips and partners who are starting to share the responsibility, but apparently not. I read recently that housekeeping requirements have actually *risen* since our grandmothers' times, and the problem is compounded by all those cooking shows that insist we source and drizzle truffle oil on everything, so that instead of just knocking up something very basic, we feel the need to be domestic goddesses. Yet a happy home is simply that – happy. Sometimes it tastes of truffle oil and sometimes of takeaway pizza; sometimes pillow cases match the duvet cover and sometimes they don't. So don't lose perspective. Feeling relaxed and positive about yourself will contribute a lot more to your home than any three-course gourmet meal ever could.

Perfection

Like unicorns and effective cellulite creams, perfection does not exist, and if 'having it all' is your definition of success you are setting yourself up for failure. So don't put yourself under pressure, constantly trying to prove your worth by being what you think others want you to be; because, ultimately, living up to so many expectations means that you end up losing sight of who you are. And isn't it better to love and revel in being a real version of an imperfect *you*, rather than a fake version of who you think you ought to be?

To sum up, the following ten tips encapsulate the essence of what a twenty-something twenty-first-century woman should always remember:

1. Be yourself.
2. There's no such thing as perfect.
3. Experiment while you're young.
4. Be media-savvy.
5. Be brave.
6. Be kind to yourself – and others.
7. Don't fear mistakes.
8. Practise good self-care.
9. Plans change – embrace that and be adaptable.
10. Invest in real friendships.

And, of course, have the time of your life! After all, whose life is it anyway?

References

Chapter 1

1. Office for National Statistics, *Annual Survey of Hours and Earnings* (2012), released 12 December 2013.
2. United States Census Bureau, *Income, Poverty and Health Insurance Coverage in the United States* (2012), released 17 September 2013.
3. D. L. Spar, *Wonder Women: Sex, Power, and the Quest for Perfection*, Sarah Crichton Books (2013).
4. Centers for Disease Control and Prevention, 'Morbidity and mortality weekly report', 17 March 2013. Accessed online at http://www.cdc.gov/mmwr/.
5. 'Do men or women worry more', nationwide survey of 1,600 adults conducted in 2006 for a consortium that included the American Psychological Association, the National Women's Health Resource Center and iVillage. Accessed online at abc.com.
6. M. Dowd, 'Get off of your cloud', *New York Times*, 26 February 2013.
7. R. O. Frost and G. Steketee, 'Perfectionism in obsessive–compulsive disorder patients', *Behaviour Research and Therapy*, 35(4) (1997), pp. 291–6; K. A. Halmi, F. Tozzi, L. M. Thornton, S. Crow, M. M. Fichter *et al.*, 'The relation among perfectionism, obsessive–compulsive personality disorder and obsessive–compulsive disorder in individuals with eating disorders', *International Journal of Eating Disorders*, 38 (2005), pp. 371–4; P. L. Hewitt and G. L. Flett, 'Dimensions of perfectionism in unipolar depression', *Journal of Abnormal Psychology*, 100(1) (1991), pp. 98–101; P. L. Hewitt, G. L. Flett and E. Ediger, 'Perfectionism and depression: longitudinal assessment of a specific vulnerability hypothesis', *Journal of Abnormal Psychology*, 105(2) (1996), pp. 276–80.

Chapter 2

1. APA Task Force on Advertising and Children, *Report of the APA Task Force on Advertising and Children* (2004). Accessed online at http://www.apa.org/pi/women/programs/girls/report.aspx

2. L. Papadopoulos, 'Sexualisation of young people', report for the UK Home Office (2010).

3. V. Ainley and M. Tsakiris, 'Body conscious? Interoceptive awareness, measured by heartbeat perception, is negatively correlated with self-objectification', *PloS ONE*, 8(2) (2013). Accessed online at http://www.plosone.org/article/info%3Adoi%2F10.1371%2F journal.pone.0055568.

4. J. J. Muehlenkamp and R. N. Saris-Baglama, 'Self objectification and its psychological outcomes for college women', *Psychology of Women Quarterly*, 26(4) (2002), pp. 371–9; B. Moradi and Y. Huang, 'Objectification theory and psychology of women: a decade of advances and future directions', *Psychology of Women Quarterly*, 32(4) (2008), pp. 377–98.

5. C. Gordon (ed), *Power/Knowledge: Selected Interviews and Other Writings 1972–1977*, Pantheon Books, New York (1980).

6. Catherine Sanderson, Amherst College, cited by Hara Estroff Marano, 'The Skinny Sweepstakes', *Psychology Today*, 1 January 2008.

7. K. E. Nintzel and C. A. Sanderson, '"But that's what all my friends think": the effect of small group membership on women's perceived discrepancy from weight-related norms', poster presented at the 5th Annual Meeting of the Society for Personality and Social Psychology, Austin, TX (2004).

8. J. L. Mensinger, D. Z. Bonifazi and J. LaRosa, 'Perceived gender role prescriptions in schools, the superwoman ideal, and disordered eating among adolescent girls', *Sex Roles*, 57(7/8) (2007), pp. 557–68.

9. G. Miller, *The Mating Mind: How Sexual Choice Shaped the Evolution of Human Nature*, First Anchor Books (2001).

10. G. Fouts and K. Vaughan, 'Television situation comedies: male weight, negative references, and audience reactions', *Sex Roles*, 46(11/12) (2002), pp. 439–42.

11. M. Tiggemann, 'Television and adolescent body image: the role of program content and viewing motivation', *Journal of Social and Clinical Psychology*, 24(3) (2005), pp. 361–81.

12. Girl Scout Research Institute, 'Real to me: girls and reality TV' (2011).

13. S. L. Smith and C. A. Cook, 'Gender stereotypes: an analysis of popular films and TV', report for the Geena Davis Institute for Gender and Media, Los Angeles (2008); 'Young Canadians in a Wired World, Phase III: Encountering Racist and Sexist Content Online', Center for Media and Digital Literacy, June 2014.

14. J. R. Goodman, 'Mapping the sea of eating disorders: a structural equation model of how peers, family, and media influence body image and eating disorders', *Visual Communication Quarterly*, 12 (2005), pp. 194–213.

15. D. Hargreaves, 'Idealized women in TV ads make girls feel bad', *Journal of Social and Clinical Psychology*, 21 (2002), pp. 287–308; R. Botta, 'For your health? The relationship between magazine

reading and adolescents' body image and eating disturbances', *Sex Roles*, 48 (2003), pp. 389–99; R. L. Vartanian, C. L. Giant and R. M. Passino, 'Ally McBeal vs. Arnold Schwarzenegger: comparing mass media, interpersonal feedback and gender as predictors of satisfaction with body thinness and muscularity', *Social Behaviour and Personality*, 29 (2001), pp. 711–24.

16. L. Wade, 'You'll be shocked at what these editors are editing out of their photos', *Huffington Post*, 8 March 2014.

17. H. Fielding, *Bridget Jones: Mad about the Boy*, Knopf, Canada (2014).

18. L. Papadopoulos, R. Bor and C. Legg, 'Coping with the disfiguring effects of vitiligo: a preliminary investigation into the effects of cognitive-behavioural therapy', *British Journal of Medical Psychology*, 72 (1999), pp. 385–96.

19. P. Sheldon, 'Pressure to be perfect: influences on college students' body esteem', *Southern Communication Journal*, 75(3) (2010), pp. 277–98.

20. D. Garner, 'Survey says: body image poll results, plagued by body image issues? The results of a national survey show you're not alone', *Psychology Today*, 1 February 1997.

21. N. Nicali, K. W. Hagberg, I. Peterson and J. I. Treasure, 'The incidence of eating disorders in the UK in 2000–2009: findings from the General Practice research database', *BMJ Open* 3(5) (2013). Accessed online at http://bmjopen.bmj.com/content/3/5/e002646.full?rss=1.

22. D. Garner, 'Survey says: body image poll results, plagued by body image issues? The results of a national survey show you're not alone', *Psychology Today*, 1 February 1997.

23. Ibid

24. W. Lassek, M. D Gaulin and S. Gaulin, 'Why women need fat: how "healthy" food makes us gain excess weight and the surprising solution to losing it forever', *Psychology Today* blog (2012). Accessed online at http://www.psychologytoday.com/ blog/why-women-need-fat.

25. Ibid.; D. Garner, 'Survey says: body image poll results, plagued by body image issues? The results of a national survey show you're not alone', *Psychology Today*, 1 February 1997.

26. J. Rodin, 'Body mania: there is growing concern with appearance, body shape, and weight, and it is a very costly pursuit: still, it's possible to get out of the body trap', *Psychology Today* (1992). Accessed online at http://www.psychologytoday.com/articles/199201/body-mania.

27. E. Reidy, 'Students spend over £1,000 a year on beauty products, *The Huffington Post UK*, 19 November 2013.

28. 'Pots of promise', *The Economist*, published online 22 May, 2003.

29. T. D. Wade and M. Tiggemann, 'The role of perfectionism in body dissatisfaction', *Journal of Eating Disorders*, 1(1) (2013). Accessed online at http://www.jeatdisord.com/content/1/1/2.

30. S. Hong, E. Tandoc Jr., E. A. Kim, B. Kim and K. Wise, 'The real you? The role of visual cues and comment congruence in perceptions of social attractiveness from Facebook profiles', *Cyberpsychology Behaviour and Social Networking*, 15(7) (2012), pp. 339–44; S. Hong, 'Facebook profile pictures influence perceived attractiveness, MU study finds', *Cyberpsychology, Behavior and Social Networking*, 12 September 2012.
31. American Academy of Facial Plastic and Reconstructive Surgery, 'Annual AAFPRS survey finds "selfie" trend increases demand for facial plastic surgery', presentation to the 11th AAFPRS International Symposium, New York City, 27–31 May 2014.

Chapter 3
1. E. Kross, P. Verduyn, E. Demiralp, J. Park, D. Seungjae Lee, N. Lin, H. Shablack, J. Jonides and O. Ybarra, 'Facebook use predicts declines in subjective well-being in young adults', *PLoS ONE*, 8(8) (2013). Accessed online at http://www.plosone.org/ article/info%3Adoi%2F10.1371%2Fjournal.pone.0069841.
2. J. Taylor, *Raising Generation Tech: Preparing Your Children for a Media-fueled World*, SourceBooks (2012).
3. S. Hong, E. Tandoc Jr., E. A. Kim, B. Kim and K. Wise, 'The real you? The role of visual cues and comment congruence in perceptions of social attractiveness from Facebook profiles', *Cyberpsychology Behaviour and Social Networking*, 15(7) (2012), pp. 339–44.
4. Ibid.
5. H. W. Marsh, U. Trautwein, O. Lüdtke and O. Köller, 'Social comparison and big-fish–little-pond effects on self-concept and other self-belief constructs: role of generalized and specific others', under review.
6. T. A. Wills, 'Downward comparison principles in social psychology', *Psychological Bulletin*, 90(2) (1981), p. 245.
7. H. W. Marsh, U. Trautwein, O. Lüdtke and O. Köller, 'Social comparison and big-fish–little-pond effects on self-concept and other self-belief constructs: role of generalized and specific others', under review; A. Tesser, M. Millar and J. Moore, 'Some affective consequences of social comparison and reflection processes: the pain and pleasure of being close', *Journal of Personality and Social Psychology*, 54(1) (1988), p. 49.
8. E. Ashikali and H. Dittmar, 'The effect of priming materialism on women's responses to thin-ideal media', *British Journal of Social Psychology*, 51(4) (2012), pp. 514–33; R. N. Ata, J. K. Thompson and B. J. Small, 'Effects of exposure to thin-ideal media images on body dissatisfaction: testing the inclusion of a disclaimer versus warning label', *Body Image*, 10(4) (2013), pp. 472–80; H. A. Hausenblas, A. Campbell, J. E. Menzel, J. Doughty, M. Levine and J. K. Thompson, 'Media effects of experimental presentation of the ideal physique on eating disorder symptoms: a meta-analysis

of laboratory studies', *Clinical Psychology Review*, 33(1) (2013), pp. 168–81.

9. 'Research spotlight on single-gender education', *NEA Reviews of the Research on Best Practices in Education*. Accessed online at http://www.nea.org/tools/17061.htm

10. A. Booth, L. Cardona-Sosa and P. Nolen, 'Gender differences in risk aversion: do single-sex environments affect their development?', *Journal of Economic Behavior & Organization*, 99(C) (2014), pp. 126–54.

11. W. Ding , F. Murray and T. Stuart, 'From bench to board: gender differences in university scientists', *Academy of Management Journal*, 56(5) (2013), pp. 1443–64.

12. J. Barsh and L. Yee, 'Unlocking the full potential of women in the US economy', special report for the *Wall Street Journal* Executive Task Force for Women in the Economy, McKinsey and Co. (2011).

13. S. Sandberg, *Lean In: Women, Work, and the Will to Lead*, Random House (2013); Why We Have Too Few Women Leaders, TED Talk, December 2010, http://www.ted.com/talks/sheryl_ sandberg_ why_we_have_too_few_women_leaders1.

14. I. M. Latu , M. S. Mast, J. Lammers, D. Bombari, 'Successful female leaders empower women's behavior in leadership tasks', *Journal of Experimental Social Psychology*, 49(3) (2013), pp. 444–48.

15. G. J. Hitsch, A. Hortaçsu, D. Ariely, 'What makes you click?— mate preferences in online dating', *Quantitative Marketing and Economics*, 8(4) (2010), pp. 393–427.

Chapter 4

1. Accessed online at http://www.simplypsychology.org/carl-rogers.html#selfw.

2. E. Svoboda 'Field guide to the people-pleaser: may I serve as your doormat? Why are some people so focused on pleasing others that they sacrifice their own needs?', *Psychology Today* (2008). Accessed online at http://www.psychologytoday.com/articles/ 200805/field-guide-the-people-pleaser-may-i-serve-your-doormat.

3. Ibid.

4. W.H. Courtenay, 'Constructions of masculinity and their influence on men's well-being: a theory of gender and health' (2000). Accessed online at pingpong.ki.se/public/pp/public_courses/ course07443/published/1295951502373/resourceId/4292165/ content/courtenay[1].pdf.

5. E. Svoboda 'Field guide to the people-pleaser: may I serve as your doormat? Why are some people so focused on pleasing others that they sacrifice their own needs?', *Psychology Today* (2008). Accessed online at http://www.psychologytoday.com/articles/ 200805/field-guide-the-people-pleaser-may-i-serve-your-doormat.

6. J. J. Exline, L. A. Zell, E. Bratslavsky, M. Hamilton and A. Swenson, 'People-pleasing through eating: sociotropy predicts

greater eating in response to perceived social pressure', *Journal of Social and Clinical Psychology*, 31(2) (2012), pp. 169–93.

7. D. D. Schwartz, 'Nice girls can finish first: getting the results you want and the respect you deserve ... while still being liked', *Huffington Post* (2009). Accessed online at http://www.huffington-post.com/daylle-deanna-schwartz/people-pleaser_b_ 1125847.html.

8. PsyArticles, 'Women Feel More Guilt'. Accessed online at http://www.psyarticles.com/values/guilt.htm.

9. C. Cryder, C. Morewedge and S. Springer, 'What does guilt do?', Ulterior Motives blog, *Psychology Today* (2012). Accessed online at http://www.psychologytoday.com/blog/ulterior-motives/ 201205/what-does-guilt-do.

10. S. Biali, 'Boundaries: it's time to say no when you need to, Prescriptions for Life blog, *Psychology Today* (2013). Accessed online at http://www.psychologytoday.com/blog/prescriptions-life/201301/boundaries-its-time-say-no-when-you-need; H. B. Braiker, *The Disease to Please: Curing the People-Pleasing Syndrome*, McGraw-Hill Education (2002).

11. The Global Entrepreneurship Monitor, *Women's Report* (2012), jointly sponsored by Babson College, US, Universidad del Desarrollo, Chile, and Universiti Tun Abdul Razak, Malaysia. Accessed online at http://www.entrepreneur.com/article/ 227631#ixzz2jhbrKLKl.

12. A. Fels, 'Do women lack ambition?', *Harvard Business Review*, April 2004; Sheryl Sandberg, *Woman's Hour* interview (2013). Accessed online at http://blog.womenreturners.com/2013/07/do-all-working-mothers-have-to-feel.html.

13. Sheryl Sandberg, *Lean In: Women, Work, and the Will to Lead*, Random House (2013).

14. M. S. Horner, 'Sex differences in achievement motivation and performance in competitive and noncompetitive situations', Ph.D. dissertation, University of Michigan (1968); M.S. Horner, 'Toward an understanding of achievement-related conflicts in women', *Journal of Social Issues*, 28 (1972), pp. 157–75.

15. J. Balkin, 'Contributions of friends to women's fear of success in college', *Psychological Reports*, 61 (1987), pp. 39–42.

16. V. Hey, *The Company She Keeps: An Ethnography of Girls' Friendship*, Open University Press (1997).

17. Tara Siegel Bernard, 'Financial advice by women, for women', *New York Times*, 23 April 2010. Accessed online at http://www. nytimes.com/2010/04/24/your-money/24money.html.

18. D. M. Sadker and M. Sadker, *Teachers, Schools, and Society*, McGraw-Hill (2004).

19. RBS survey (2013). Accessed online at http://www.theinformation daily.com/2013/10/17/fear-of-failure-stops-women-from-starting-their-own-business.

20. N. Wolf, *The Beauty Myth: How Images of Beauty Are Used against Women*, William Morrow and Company (1992).

21. S. Hinshaw and R. Kranz, *The Triple Bind Saving Our Teenage Girls from Today's Pressures and Conflicting Expectations*, Random House (2009).
22. M. Leicester and S. Modgil, *Moral Education and Pluralism*, Routledge (1999).
23. Office for National Statistics, *Mental Health in Children and Young People in Great Britain* (2005).

Chapter 5
1. J. Kilbourne, *Killing Us Softly 4: Advertising's Image of Women*, documentary, Media Education Foundation (2010).
2. C. Heldman, 'The sexy lie', Ted Talk (2013). Accessed online at http://www.youtube.com/watch?v=kMS4VJKekW8.
3. L. Papadopoulos, 'Sexualisation of young people', report for the UK Home Office (2010).
4. D. Merskin, 'Reviving Lolita? A media literacy examination of sexual portrayals of girls in fashion and advertising', *American Behavioural Scientist*, 48 (2004), p. 119.
5. C. Heldman, 'The sexy lie', Ted Talk (2013). Accessed online at http://www.youtube.com/watch?v=kMS4VJKekW8.
6. J. Kilbourne, *Killing Us Softly 4: Advertising's Image of Women*, documentary, Media Education Foundation (2010).
7. 'GroupM forecasts 2012 global ad spending to increase 6.4%', according to communications services group WPP (5 December 2011). Accessed online at http://www.groupm.com/pressandnews.
8. M. S. Kimmel, *The Gendered Society*, Oxford University Press USA (2008).
9. P. R. Sanday, *Fraternity Gang Rape: Sex, Brotherhood, and Privilege on Campus*, New York University Press (2007).
10. J. Ropelato, internet pornography statistics (2006), as cited in L. Papadopoulos, 'Sexualisation of young people', report for the UK Home Office (2010).
11. M. Zook, 'Report on the location of the internet adult industry', in K. Jacobs, M. Janssen and M. Pasquinelli (eds), *C'lick Me: A Netporn Studies Reader*, Institute of Network Culture (2007), pp. 103–24.
12. A. Bandura, 'Social learning theory of aggression', in J. F. Knutson (ed.), *The Control of Aggression: Implications from Basic Research*, Aldine (1973), pp. 201–50.
13. A. J. Bridges, R. Wosnitzer, E. Scharrer, C. Sun and R. Liberman, 'Aggression and sexual behavior in best-selling pornography videos: a content analysis update', *Violence against Women* (in press).
14. D. Loftus, *Watching Sex: How Men Really Respond to Pornography*, Thunder's Mouth Press (2002); R. Bauserman, 'Sexual aggression and pornography: a review of correlational research', *Basic and Applied Social Psychology*, 18 (1996), pp. 405–27; N. M. Malamuth and E. Donnerstein (eds), *Pornography and Sexual Aggression*, Academic Press Inc. (1984), pp. 19–52.

15. D. L. Mosher and P. Maclan, 'College men and women respond to X-rated videos intended for male or female audiences: gender and sexual scripts', *Journal of Sex Research*, 31 (1994), pp. 99–113.
16. R. J. Wosnitzer and A. J. Bridges 'Aggression and sexual behavior in best-selling pornography: a content analysis update', paper presented at the 57th Annual Meeting of the International Communication Association, San Francisco, CA, 2007.
17. J. Kilbourne, *Killing Us Softly 4: Advertising's Image of Women*, documentary, Media Education Foundation (2010).
18. J. Johnson, M. Adams, L. Ashburn and W. Reed, 'Differential gender effects of exposure to rap music on African American adolescents' acceptance of teen dating violence', *Sex Roles*, 33 (1995), pp. 597–605.
19. Nicholas Carr, *The Shallows: What the Internet Is Doing to Our Brains*, W. W. Norton (2010); Clive Thompson, *Smarter Than You Think: How Technology Is Changing Our Minds for the Better*, Penguin Press (2013).
20. T. Wu, 'The problem with easy technology', *New Yorker* blog, February 2014. Accessed online at http://www.newyorker.com/online/blogs/elements/2014/02/the-problem-with-easy-technology.html.
21. Ibid.
22. BBC News Online, Thursday, 26 November 2009.
23. J. Ringrose, R. Gill, S. Livingstone and L. Harvey, 'A qualitative study of children, young people and "sexting"', report for the NSPCC (2012).
24. L. M. Carpenter, 'From girls into women: scripts for sexuality and romance in *Seventeen* magazine, 1974–1994', *Journal of Sex Research*, 35 (1998), pp. 158–68; M. Durham, 'Dilemmas of desire: representations of adolescent sexuality in two teen magazines', *Youth and Society*, 29 (1998), pp. 369–89; A. Garner, H. M. Strek and S. Adams, 'Narrative analysis of sexual etiquette in teenage magazines, *Journal of Communication*, 48 (1998), pp. 59–78.
25. A. Phippen, 'Sexting: an exploration of practices, attitudes and influences', report for the NSPCC/UK Safer Internet Centre (2012).
26. A. Lenhart, 'How and why minor teens are sending sexually suggestive nude or nearly nude images via text messaging', report for the Pew Internet and American Life Project (an initiative of the Pew Research Center) (2005); J. Ringrose, R. Gill, S. Livingstone and L. Harvey, 'A qualitative study of children, young people and "sexting"', report for the NSPCC (2012).
27. A. Phippen, 'Sexting: an exploration of practices, attitudes and influences', report for the NSPCC/UK Safer Internet Centre (2012).
28. J. Ringrose, R. Gill, S. Livingstone and L. Harvey, 'A qualitative study of children, young people and "sexting"', report for the NSPCC (2012).
29. J. D. Brown and K. L. L'Engle, 'X-rated: sexual attitudes and behav-

iors associated with US early adolescents' exposure to sexually explicit media', *Communication Research*, 36 (2009), pp. 129–51; A. Phippen, 'Sexting: an exploration of practices, attitudes and influences', report for the NSPCC/UK Safer Internet Centre (2012).

30. L. Papadopoulos, 'Sexualisation of young people', report for the UK Home Office; J. Ringrose, 'Every time she bends over she pulls up her thong: teen girls negotiating discourses of competitive, heterosexualised aggression', *Girlhood Studies: An Interdisciplinary Journal*, 1(1) (2008): pp. 33–59; J. Ringrose, 'Just be friends: exposing the limits of educational bully discourses for understanding teen girls' heterosexualized friendships and conflicts', *British Journal of Sociology of Education*, 29(5) (2008), pp. 509–22.

31. M. Martinez and T. Manolovitz 'Incest, sexual violence and rape in video games' (2009). Accessed online at http://www.inter-disciplinary.net/wp-content/uploads/2009/06/incest-sexual-violence-and-rape-in-video-games.pdf.

32. C. Rodenberg, 'Grand Theft Auto V makes it cool to pick up – even kill – prostitutes', *Guardian*, 27 December 2013. Accessed online at http://www.theguardian.com/commentisfree/2013/dec/27/grand-theft-auto-v-prostitutes-killed?CMP=fb_us.

33. Quoted in M. T. Reist (ed.), *Getting Real: Challenging the Sexualisation of Girls*, Spinifex Press (2009).

34. M. Locker, 'California school bans leggings because they were distracting to boys', *Time*, 15 April 2013. Accessed online at http://newsfeed.time.com/2013/04/15/california-school-bans-leggings-because-they-were-distracting-to-boys/. According to the school's principal, 'When girls bend in leggings the threads spread and that's really when it becomes a problem.'

35. J. Kilbourne, *Killing Us Softly 4: Advertising's Image of Women*, documentary, Media Education Foundation (2010).

Chapter 6

1. A. Campbell, *Staying Alive: Evolution, Culture, and Women's Intrasexual Aggression*, Cambridge University Press (1999); T. Vaillancourt, 'Do human females use indirect aggression as an intrasexual competition strategy?', *Philosophical Transactions of the Royal Society*, 368(1631) (2013). Accessed online at http://rstb.royalsocietypublishing.org/content/368/1631/20130080.full.pdf+html.

2. M. Billig and H. Tajfel, 'Social categorization and similarity in intergroup behaviour', *European Journal of Social Psychology*, 3(1) (1973), pp. 27–52.

3. J. E. Workman and S. H. Lee, 'Relationships among consumer vanity, gender, brand sensitivity, brand consciousness and private self-consciousness', *International Journal of Consumer Studies*, 37 (2013), pp. 206–13.

4. S. E. Asch, 'Effects of group pressure on the modification and distortion of judgments', in H. Guetzkow (ed.), *Groups, Leadership and Men*, Carnegie Press (1951), pp. 177–90.

5. E. Aronson and J. Mills, 'The effect of severity of initiation on liking for a group', *Journal of Abnormal and Social Psychology*, 59 (1959), pp. 177–81.

6. A. James, 'School Bullying', unpublished report for the NSPCC (2010).

7. D. Olweus, *Bullying at School: What We Know and What We Can Do*, Blackwell Publishing (1993).

8. R. Simmons, *Odd Girl Out: The Hidden Culture of Aggression in Girls*, Harcourt (2002).

9. K. M. J. Lagerspetz, K. Bjorkqvist and T. Peltonen, 'Is indirect aggression more typical of females? Gender differences in aggressiveness in 11–12 year old children', *Aggressive Behavior*, 14 (1988), pp. 403–14.

10. K. Bjorkqvist and P. Niemela, 'New trends in the study of female aggression', in K. Bjorkqvist and P. Niemela (eds), *Mice and Women: Aspects of Female Aggression*, Academic Press (1992), pp. 3–15.

11. N. R. Crick and J. K. Grotpeter, 'Relational aggression, gender, and social psychological adjustment', *Child Development*, 66 (3) (1995), pp. 710–22; N. R Crick and J. K. Grotpeter, 'Children's maltreatment by peers: victims of relational aggression', *Development and Psychopathology*, 8 (1996), pp. 367–80.

12. L. M. Brown, *Raising Their Voices: The Politics of Girls' Anger*, Harvard University Press (1998).

13. G. Namie, 2010 Workplace bullying survey, Workplace Bullying Institute. Accessed online at http://www.workplacebullying.org/.

14. N. R. Crick and A. J. Rose, 'Toward a gender-balanced approach to the study of social-emotional development: a look at relational aggression', in P. H. Miller and E. Kofsky Scholnick (eds), *Toward a Feminist Developmental Psychology*, Taylor & Frances/Routledge (2000), pp. 153–68.

15. C. Dellasegam and C. Nixon, *Girl Wars: 12 Strategies That Will End Female Bullying*, Fireside (2003).

16. R. Wiseman, *Queen Bees and Wannabes: Helping Your Daughter Survive Cliques, Gossip, Boyfriends, and Other Realities of Adolescence*, Crown Publishers (2002).

17. C. Moore, *Margaret Thatcher: The Authorized Biography*, Volume One: *Not for Turning*, Allen Lane (2013).

18. J. Ringrose, 'A new universal mean girl: examining the discursive construction and social regulation of a new feminine pathology', *Feminism Psychology*, 16(405) (2006). Accessed online at http://www.academia.edu/332020/A_New_Universal_ Mean_Girl_ Examining_the_Discursive_Construction_and_Social_Regulation_of _a_New_Feminine_Pathology.

19. M. M. Duguid, 'Female tokens in high-prestige work groups: catalysts or inhibitors of group diversification?', *Organizational Behavior and Human Decision Processes Journal*, 116(1) (2011), pp. 104–115.

20. T. Vaillancourt, 'Do human females use indirect aggression as an

intrasexual competition strategy?', *Philosophical Transactions of the Royal Society*, 368(1631) (2013). Accessed online at http://rstb.royal societypublishing.org/content/368/1631/20130080.full.pdf+html.

21. J. Archer, 'Sex differences in aggression in real-world settings: a meta-analytic review', *Review of General Psychology*, 8 (2004), pp. 291–322.

22. P. Stockley and A. Campbell, 'Introduction: female competition and aggression: interdisciplinary perspectives', *Philosophical Transactions of the Royal Society*, 368(1631) (2013). Accessed online at http://rstb.royalsocietypublishing.org/content/368/ 1631/2013 0073.full.pdf; J. F. Benenson 'The development of human female competition: allies and adversaries', *Philosophical Transactions of the Royal Society*, 368(1631) (2013). Accessed online at http://rstb. royalsocietypublishing.org/content/368/ 1631/20130079.full.pdf +html; A. Campbell, 'The evolutionary psychology of women's aggression', *Philosophical Transactions of the Royal Society*, 368(1631) (2013). Accessed online at http://rstb.royalsocietypub-lishing.org/content/368/1631/ 20130078.long.

23. T. Vaillancourt, 'Do human females use indirect aggression as an intrasexual competition strategy?', *Philosophical Transactions of the Royal Society*, 368(1631) (2013). Accessed online at http:// rstb.roy-alsocietypublishing.org/content/368/1631/20130080.full.pdf+html.

24. A. Campbell, 'The evolutionary psychology of women's aggres-sion', *Philosophical Transactions of the Royal Society*, 368(1631) (2013). Accessed online at http://rstb.royalsocietypublishing.org/ content/368/1631/20130078.long.

25. NSPCC statistics on bullying collated from government reports and research. Accessed online at http://www.NSPCC.org (2013); Ofcom, 'Children and parents: media use and attitudes', report (2013).

26. R. Wiseman, *Queen Bees and Wannabes: Helping Your Daughter Survive Cliques, Gossip, Boyfriends, and Other Realities of Adolescence*, Crown Publishers (2002).

27. J. Miller, *One of the Guys: Girls, Gangs, and Gender*, Oxford University Press York (2001).

28. M. Flood, 'Male and female sluts: shifts and stabilities in the reg-ulation of sexual relations among young heterosexual men', *Australian Feminist Studies*, 28(75) (2013), pp. 95–107.

29. J. Kitzinger, '"I'm sexually attractive but I'm powerful": young women negotiating sexual reputation', *Women's Studies International Forum*, 18(2) (1995), pp. 187–96.

30. B. Younger, *Learning Curves: Body Image and Female Sexuality in Young Adult Literature*, Scarecrow Studies in Young Adult Literature, The Scarecrow Press Inc. (2009); L. Tanenbaum, *Slut! Growing up Female with a Bad Reputation*, Perennial (2000).

31. D. Kreager and J. Staff, 'The sexual double standard and adoles-cent peer acceptance', *Social Psychology Quarterly*, 72 (2009), pp. 143–64; L. Tanenbaum, *Slut! Growing up Female with a Bad Reputation*, Perennial (2000).

32. J. Kitzinger, '"I'm sexually attractive but I'm powerful": young women negotiating sexual reputation', *Women's Studies International Forum*, 18(2) (1995), pp. 187–96.
33. T. Vaillancourt and A. Sharma, 'Intolerance of sexy peers: intra-sexual competition among women', *Aggressive Behavior*, 37 (2011), pp. 569–577.
34. K. Stamoulis, 'Why girls call each other sluts', The New Teen Age blog, *Psychology Today*, 12 October 2012. Accessed online at http://www.psychologytoday.com/blog/the-new-teen-age/201210/why-girls-call-each-other-sluts.
35. L. Papadopoulos, 'Sexualisation of young people', report for the UK Home Office (2010).
36. K. Weir, 'Fickle friends: how to deal with frenemies', *Scientific American*, 14 April 2011. Accessed online at http://www.scientificamerican.com/article/fickle-friends/.
37. J. Holt-Lunstad, B. N. Uchino, T. W. Smith, C. B. Cerny and J. B. Nealey-Moore, 'Social relationships and ambulatory blood pressure: structural and qualitative predictors of cardiovascular function during everyday social interactions', *Health Psychology*, 22 (2003), pp. 388–97.
38. B. N. Uchino, J. Holt-Lunstad , D. Uno and J.B. Flinders 'Heterogeneity in the social networks of young and older adults: prediction of mental health and cardiovascular reactivity during acute stress', *Journal of Behavioural Medicine*, 24(4) (2001), pp. 361–82.
39. L. M. Brown, *Raising Their Voices: The Politics of Girls' Anger*, Harvard University Press (1998); L. M. Brown, *Girlfighting: Betrayal and Rejection among Girls*, New York University Press (2003); R. Simmons, *Odd Girl Out: The Hidden Culture of Aggression in Girls*, Harcourt (2002).

Chapter 7

1. E. Furman, *Boomerang Nation: How to Survive Living with Your Parents . . . the Second Time Around*, Touchstone (2005).
2. J. J. Arnett, *Emerging Adulthood: The Winding Road from the Late Teens through the Twenties*, Oxford University Press (2000).
3. Ibid.; J. J. Arnett, 'Conceptions of the transition to adulthood: perspectives from adolescence through midlife', *Journal of Adult Development*, 8(2) (2001). Accessed online at http://www.jeffreyarnett.com/articles/ARNETT_conceptions_of_the_transition_to_adulthood.pdf; Chartered Institute of Personnel and Development, 'High number of graduates moving into unrelated employment risks creating a "disillusioned generation" – and excessive targets risk making the matter worse', press release, 29 March 2010. Accessed online at http://www.cipd. co.uk/pressoffice/press-releases/graduates-unrelated-employment.aspx.
4. E. Sharp and L. Ganong, '"I'm a loser, I'm not married, let's all just look at me": ever-single women's perceptions of their social environment', *Journal of Family Issues*, 20 January 2011.

5. B. Headey, R. Muffels and G. G. Wagner, 'Long-running German panel survey shows that personal and economic choices, not just genes, matter for happiness', *Proceedings of the National Academy of Sciences of the United States of America* , 31 August, 2010. Accessed online at http://www.pnas.org/content/107/42/17922.abstract? sid=81051852-6732-4688-b01c-72357 e13389d.
6. Rosamund Irwin, 'Today's female role models', *Huffington Post*, 2 April 2013. Accessed online at http://www.huffingtonpost. co.uk/2013/02/04/girls-series-1-exclusive-clip-rosamund-irwin_n_2614273.html; Anita Sheth, 'Regrets? I've had a few', *Glamour*, 4 February 2013. Accessed online at http://www.glamour magazine.co.uk/features/relationships/2013/02/oops-i-did-it-again.
7. C. Thompson, 'Brave New World of Digital Intimacy', *New York Times Magazine*, 5 September 2008. Accessed online at http://www.nytimes.com/2008/09/07/magazine/07awareness-t. html?pagewanted=all&_r=0.
8. J. DiMicco, D. R. Millen, W. Geyer, C. Dugan, B. Brownholtz and M. Muller, 'Motivations for social networking at work', IBM Research (2008). Accessed online at http://www.umsl.edu/~ sauterv/5800/p711-dimicco.pdf.
9. E. Kross, P. Verduyn, E. Demiralp, J. Park, S. E. Lee, N. Lin, H. Shablack, J. Jonides and O. Ybarra, 'Facebook use predicts declines in subjective well-being in young adults' *PLoS ONE*, 8(8) (2013). Accessed online at http://www.plosone.org/article/info%3Adoi% 2F10.1371%2Fjournal.pone.0069841.
10. Jonathan Safran Foer, 'How Not to Be Alone', *The New York Times Sunday Review* , 8 June, 2013.

Chapter 8

1. Havas Worldwide Prosumer, 'Aging: moving beyond youth culture', report (2012).
2. American Psychological Society, 'Stress in America™: missing the health care connection', survey (2013). Accessed online at https:// www.apa.org/news/press/releases/stress/2012/full-report.pdf.
3. M. Standish, 'Millennials' youth obsession is stressing them out', *HuffPost Healthy Living*, 3 April 2013. Accessed online at http://www.huffingtonpost.com/maude-standish/millennials-youth-obsessi_b_3001138.html.
4. J. M. Twenge and W. K. Campbell, *The Narcissism Epidemic: Living in the Age of Entitlement*, Simon & Schuster (2009); R. Baumeister, *Self-esteem: The Puzzle of Low Self-regard*, Plenum Series in Social/Clinical Psychology, Kluwer Academic/Plenum (1993).
5. J. Stein, 'Millennials: the me me me generation', *Time*, 20 May 2013.
6. C. Newport, *So Good They Can't Ignore You: Why Skills Trump Passion in the Quest for Work You Love*, Grand Central Publishing (2012).
7. Alison Herman, 'Why Generation Y yuppies are unhappy', *Huffington Post*, 15 September 2013.

8. C. Newport, *So Good They Can't Ignore You: Why Skills Trump Passion in the Quest for Work You Love*, Grand Central Publishing (2012).

9. Ibid.

10. W. Mischel, Y. Shoda and M. L. Rodriguez, 'Delay of gratification in children', *Science*, 244 (1989), pp. 933–8.

11. Y. Shoda, W. Mischel and P. K. Peake, 'Predicting adolescent cognitive and social competence from preschool delay of gratification: identifying diagnostic conditions', *Developmental Psychology*, 26 (1990), pp. 978–86.

12. T. R. Schlam, N. L. Wilson, Y. Shoda, W. Mischel and O. Ayduk, 'Preschoolers' delay of gratification predicts their body mass 30 years later', *Journal of Pediatrics*, 162 (2013), pp. 90–3.

13. Jenny Hope and Roger Dobson, 'Children's plastic surgery epidemic', *Daily Mail Online* 2014

14. Vivian Diller, 'A solution to bullying: where do we draw the line?, *Huffington Post*, 31 July 2012.

15. Parker J. Palmer, *Let Your Life Speak: Listening for the Voice of Vocation*, Jossey-Bass (2000).

16. E. H. Erikson, *Identity: Youth and Crisis*, W. W. Norton (1968).

17. O. C. Robinson and G. R. T. Wright, 'The prevalence, types and perceived outcomes of crisis episodes in early adulthood and midlife: a structured retrospective-autobiographical study', *International Journal of Behavioural Development*, 37 (2013), pp. 407–16; O. C. Robinson, 'Values and adult age: findings from two cohorts of the European Social Survey', *European Journal of Ageing*, 10 (2013), pp. 11–23.

18. A. Przybylski, 'Motivational, well-being, and behavioral correlates of fear of missing out', *Computers in Human Behavior*, 29 April 2013.

19. Parker J. Palmer, *Faith or Frenzy*, Trinity United Methodist Church (1992).

Index